Information Sources and Searching on the World Wide Web

G G Chowdhury
Department of Information Science, University of Strathclyde

Sudatta Chowdhury
*formerly Division of Information Studies, School of Applied Science,
Nanyang Technological University, Singapore*

LIBRARY ASSOCIATION PUBLISHING
LONDON

© G G Chowdhury and Sudatta Chowdhury, 2001

Published by
Library Association Publishing
7 Ridgmount Street
London WC1E 7AE

Library Association Publishing is wholly owned by The Library Association.

First published 2001

British Library Cataloguing in Publication Data

A catalogue record for this book is available from the British Library.

ISBN 1-85604-394-0

Typeset from author's disk in 11/14pt Elegant Garamond and Humanist 521 by Library Association Publishing.
Printed and made in Great Britain by MPG Books Ltd, Bodmin, Cornwall.

To Avirup and Anubhav

Contents

Acknowledgements

In order to illustrate the content of the various chapters in this book, we have included a number of screenshots of various web information sources and services. Requests were made to the various parties for permissions to reprint the screenshots of their web pages. Fortunately, most gave us permission on time, and in this section we have acknowledged them. Whilst every effort has been made to obtain permissions, some parties did not respond to our requests. For those screenshots we have shown the source and mentioned the name of the copyright owner. Copyright owners should contact the Publishers with any queries regarding permissions or acknowledgements.

Chapter 3

Fig. 3.2: Reprinted with the kind permission of AltaVista
   http://www.altavista.com
Fig. 3.3: Reprinted with the kind permission of Google Inc.
   http://www.google.com
Fig. 3.4: Source
   http://www.alltheweb.com
   copyright Fast Search & Transfer ASA
Figs. 3.5 and 3.6: Source
   http://www.ask.co.uk
   copyright Ask Jeeves, Inc.

Chapter 4

Fig. 4.2: Source
   http://www.yahoo.com
   copyright Yahoo! Inc.

Fig. 4.3: Source

http://www.lycos.com

copyright Lycos Inc.

Fig. 4.4: Reprinted with the kind permission of LookSmart

http://www.looksmart.com

Fig. 4.5: Reprinted with the kind permission of Argus Clearinghouse

http://www.clearinghouse.net

Fig. 4.6: Reprinted with the kind permission of WWW Virtual Library

http://www.vlib.org

Chapter 5

Figs. 5.1, 5.2 and 5.3: Reprinted with the kind permission of SOSIG

http://www.sosig.ac.uk

Fig. 5.4: Reprinted with the kind permission of Biz/ed

http://www.biz.ac.uk

Figs. 5.5, 5.6, 5.7 and 5.8: Reprinted with the kind permission of EEVL

http://www.eevl.ac.uk

Figs. 5.9, 5.10, 5.11 and 5.12: Reprinted with the kind permission of EELS

http://eels.lub.lu.se/

Fig. 5.13: Reprinted with the kind permission of OMNI/BIOME

http://omni.ac.uk/

Figs. 5.14, 5.15 and 5.16: Source

http://novagate.nova-university.org/

copyright Nova University

Figs. 5.17, 5.18 and 5.19: Reprinted with the kind permission of BUBL

http://www.bubl.ac.uk

Chapter 6

Figs. 6.1 and 6.2: Source

http://www.earl.org.uk/ask/

copyright Earl: the Consortium for Public Library Networking.

Figs. 6.3, 6.4, 6.5, 6.6 and 6.7: Source

http://www1.askme.com/BusinessSplash.asp

copyright AskMe Corporation

Figs. 6.8 and 6.9: Reprinted with the kind permission of AllExperts.com

http://www.allexperts.com

Fig. 6.10: Reprinted with the kind permission of the British Library
http://www.bl.uk

Figs. 6.11 and 6.12: Reprinted with the kind permission of Nolo.com, Inc.
http://www.auntienolo.com

Figs. 6.13 and 6.14: Reprinted with the kind permission of FIND/SVP, Inc.
http://www.findsvp.com

Figs. 6.15 and 6.16: Reprinted with the kind permission of ProfessionalCity
www.ProfessionalCity.com

Figs. 6.17 and 6.18: Reprinted with the kind permission of Bartleby
http://www.bartleby.com

Figs. 6.22, 6.23 and 6.24: Source
http://www.elibrary.com
copyright Infonautics Corpn.

Figs. 6.25 and 6.26: Reprinted with the kind permission of The Learning
Network Inc.
http://www.learningnetwork.com

Figs. 6.27 and 6.28: Source
http://www.itcompany.com/inforetriever/
copyright Vianne Tang Sha InfoWorks Technology Company

Fig. 6.29: Reprinted with the kind permission of MediaEaterReference
Desk

Figs. 6.30 and 6.31: Source
http://itools.com/research-it/
copyright iTools

Chapter 7

Figs. 7.1 and 7.2: Reprinted with the kind permission of SwetsNetNavigator

Figs. 7.3 and 7.4: Reprinted with the kind permission of EBSCO Online

Figs. 7.5 and 7.6: Source
http://www.ingenta.com
copyright Ingenta

Fig. 7.7: Reprinted with the kind permission of Highwire press

Figs. 7.8, 7.9 and 7.10: Reprinted with the kind permission of IDEAL

Figs. 7.11 and 7.12: Source
http://www.dlib.org
copyright D-Lib Forum

Fig. 7.13: Source
http://ebooks.barnesandnoble.com
copyright BarnesandNoble.com

Chapter 8

Figs. 8.1 and 8.2: Reprinted with the kind permission of NCSTRL
http://cs-tr.cs.cornell.edu/

Figs. 8.3, 8.4, 8.5, 8.6 and 8.7: Reprinted with the kind permission of NDLTD/ETD
http://www.ndltd.org and http://www.theses.org

Fig. 8.8: Reprinted with the kind permission of MIT Libraries

Fig. 8.9: Reprinted with the kind permission of Alexandria Digital Library Project
http://alexandria.ucsb.edu

Fig. 8.10: Reprinted with the kind permission of NZDL
http://www.nzdl.org/

Figs. 8.11 and 8.12: Reprinted with the kind permission of the Regents of the University of California

Figs. 8.13, 8.14 and 8.15: Reprinted with the kind permission of HeadLine Project
http://www.headline.ac.uk

Preface

Over the years most information resources have appeared in electronic form – on CD-ROM, remote online databases, and more recently on the world wide web. Consequently, today's information professionals face the challenges of learning about these various electronic information sources, and also of mastering the corresponding search and retrieval techniques. In order to help information practitioners and students learn about the variety of electronic information sources vis-à-vis the information retrieval techniques, we authored a book, *Searching CD-ROM and online information sources* which was published earlier this year by Library Association Publishing. The book covers different types of electronic information sources ranging from online public access catalogues to CD-ROM and online search services, and some institutional information sources on the world wide web. However, the book did not cover a large variety of information sources that are available on the web, the various web search tools, and web-based information services. The present book aims to cover the above-mentioned area, and hence can be treated as a perfect companion to the former title.

The purpose

The major objective of this book is to give an overview of the various information sources and services available on the web, and the corresponding tools and techniques that are required to search and retrieve the information. If the user is aware of the existence of a particular website and its address, i.e. the URL (uniform resource locator) he or she can go directly to the information resource. However, if the user is in doubt about the availability of a particular piece of information on the web, or is aware that it is available but does not know where, a search tool must be used. Different types of web search tools are available. They can largely be classified as search engines, directories, virtual libraries and subject gateways. This book describes the features of these different categories of search tools.

Electronic journals available through the web now enable users to read journal information from their desk. However, the search interfaces that come with these journals often differ, so users need to learn various search techniques in order to be able to retrieve information. This book describes the features of various search and retrieval tools that are available.

Many new web-based reference and information services and digital library services have been introduced recently that also allow users to search and retrieve information from their desk. We describe the nature and characteristics of various web-based reference and information services, as well as digital libraries.

The audience

The primary objective of writing this book is to help students of library and information science, as well as practising information professionals, throughout the world learn how to use the wide variety of information sources and services that are available on the web. The book will be useful for all students and teachers taking or teaching courses on reference and/or information sources and services, information retrieval, the internet and world wide web, and so on. It will also help end-users who want to know, and make the best use of, the variety of information sources and services available on the web.

The content and approach

We begin with a general introduction to the web and its underlying technology. Although this is not the central theme of this book, and consequently it has been kept quite simple, this has been included to give readers an idea of how web pages are created and are interpreted by web browsers. Chapter 2 discusses basic search techniques, with examples drawn from various web search engines. Chapter 3 describes the basic working principles of search engines, followed by the features of selected search engines, meta search engines and special-purpose search engines. Essential features of selected search and meta search engines are presented in Table 3.1 as a ready reference source. Specific characteristics of some search engines are also discussed to help users select an appropriate search engine.

Chapter 4 discusses the working principles of web directories, a selection of which, large and small, are described. Uses of the directories are illustrated with some practical examples. Chapter 5 discusses the concept of subject gateways and describes the features of a selection of these, with appropriate examples and screenshots.

The web has made a significant impact on traditional reference services, and now a number of web-based reference services are available. While some of these services are restricted to members only, others are free and can be used by anyone. The nature of these services also varies – in some cases users can send a query to a reference librarian through the web and get the answer back in the form of e-mail, in others users can go to a website and can ask (type) the question and get the answer (the required text, image, etc.) right there. Chapter 6 discusses the features of some such web-based reference and information services with appropriate screenshots and examples.

Electronic journals have become a very important source of information available on the web. While some of these journals are the electronic counterparts of their printed versions, others are available only in electronic format. The majority of the e-journals available today either are restricted to specific users or make a charge for usage – but some are freely accessible. E-journals are available either directly from the publisher or through a vendor (called an aggregator), and there are some agencies that have taken the role of archiving e-journals. Chapter 7 describes the various means of accessing e-journals. Features of some selected aggregators, e-journals projects and publishers are described. This chapter also outlines the characteristic features of electronic books, with appropriate illustrations.

The web has been the enabling technology for another major development in the information world, namely digital libraries. Of those that are available on the web, some have restricted access while others are freely accessible to anyone. Digital libraries vary in terms of their content and characteristics, and often have different interfaces and search and retrieval techniques, which users need to be aware of in order to make optimal use of these resources. Chapter 8 describes the features of some selected digital libraries, highlighting the various ways through which users can retrieve the required information. Appropriate examples and screenshots have been added to facilitate the discussion.

As already indicated, the web has brought tremendous changes in the way we create, search for and use information in our day-to-day lives. We end with a discussion on the trends related to the various information services available on the web.

Note: Where names of websites are given in parentheses throughout the text, their full addresses are given in the list of websites beginning on page 164.

Acknowledgements

First of all we would like to express our sincere thanks to all the publishers and institutions who have given us permission to use the screenshots of their products and services as examples in this book. We would like to thank people at Library Association Publishing, London, especially Helen Carley, Lin Franklin, Helen Vaux, Kathryn Beecroft and June York, without whose constant support and help this book would not have seen the light of day.

Thanks are also due to our parents and relatives, who have always encouraged us to accomplish our task. Finally, we would like to thank our two charming sons, Avirup and Anubhav, who have always been our sources of inspiration. They have been very considerate and co-operative all through. It is our pleasure to dedicate this book to them.

G. G. Chowdhury and Sudatta Chowdhury

Chapter 1
Introduction

The web

The world wide web (WWW or simply the web) is a massive collection of pages of information, stored on millions of computers across the world that are linked by the internet. The development of the web began in 1989 with the work of Tim Berners-Lee and his colleagues at CERN (the European Laboratory for Particle Physics in Geneva). They created a protocol, called the hypertext transfer protocol (HTTP), which standardized communication between servers and clients. Their text-based browser, used to search the web, was made available for general release in January 1992. The web gained rapid acceptance with the creation of a browser called Mosaic, which was developed in the United States at the National Center for Supercomputing Applications at the University of Illinois, and was released in September 1993 (Poulter, Hiom and Tseng, 2000). Mosaic allowed people to use the web using 'point-and-click' graphical manipulations. Subsequently the Mosaic staff started their own company and developed one of the two most popular web browsers of today, Netscape Navigator. The most popular browser, Internet Explorer from Microsoft Corporation, appeared soon after.

This chapter provides a quick overview of the basic technology that governs the web. It discusses how web pages are created and are viewed by the users, with a brief introduction to hypertext markup language (HTML). These discussions will be particularly useful for beginners, and they set the background for the rest of the book.

The basic technology

Let's try to understand the basic technology that runs the web. We begin with a very simple question: what do we need to work with the web? The simple answer is:

- an internet connection, and
- a web browser.

A web browser is a computer program that does two things:

- it can access a web server on the internet, request and retrieve a page
- it interprets the set of HTML tags (see pp. 4–5) within the page, which it then displays on the user's screen.

A web browser thus deals with a web server. In general, a server is a computer that provides services to other computer programs in the same or other computers. The computer that a server program runs on is also frequently referred to as a server (though it may contain a number of server and client programs) (Server, n.d.). Client/server describes the relationship between two computer programs in which one program, the client, makes a service request from another program, the server, which fulfils the request (Client/server, n.d.). In a network, the client/server model provides a convenient way to interconnect programs that are distributed efficiently across the network.

A web server is a piece of computer software that runs on a computer connected to the internet. It can respond to a browser's request for a page, and deliver the page to the web browser through the internet. Every computer on the internet that contains, or hosts, a website must have a web server program. The most popular web servers are Microsoft's Internet Information Server, which comes with the Windows NT server, Netscape FastTrack and Enterprise servers, and Apache, a web server for UNIX-based operating systems (Web server, n.d.).

In the usual client/server model, one server, sometimes called a daemon, is activated and awaits client requests. Typically, multiple client programs share the services of a common server program. Both client programs and server programs are often part of a larger program or application. In the context of the internet, your web browser is a client program that requests services (the sending of web pages or files) from a web server (technically, a hypertext transport protocol, or hypertext transfer protocol server) in another computer somewhere on the internet. Similarly, your computer with TCP/IP (transmission control protocol/internet protocol) installed allows you to make client requests for files from file transfer protocol (FTP) servers in other computers on the internet.

The basic process

In order to access a website you need to know its file address, or URL (uniform resource locator). Suppose you type the URL **http://www.dis.strath.ac.uk/ courses/buscomp** into your browser and press <return>. Then, no matter where that website is, the page pops up on your screen.

Several things happened here behind the scene:

Step 1
The browser divided the URL into three parts:

- the protocol (**http**)
- the server name (**www.dis.strath.ac.uk**)
- the file name (**courses/buscomp**).

Step 2
The browser communicated with a domain name server (DNS) to translate the server name (**www.dis.strath.ac.uk**) into an IP address, which it uses to connect to the server machine. Each machine on the internet is assigned a unique IP address. These are 32-bit numbers normally expressed as four 'octets' in a 'dotted decimal number'. A typical IP address looks like this:

216.27.61.137

An octet is a number between 0 and 255 (2^8 possibilities per octet). A server has a static IP address that does not change very often. A home machine that uses a dial-up connection through a modem often has an IP address that is assigned by the ISP (internet service provider) when you dial in. That IP address is unique for a given session, but may be different the next time you dial in. The DNS system is a very large distributed database system that keeps track of each and every IP address on the internet. Whenever we type a URL on our browser, the browser sends a message to a DNS to get an IP address for the domain for which we have typed a URL (e.g. **strath.ac.uk**). Domain name servers not only provide the correct IP address for a domain, but also keep track of new domain names as well as changes in domain names. This massive distributed database system has possibly the largest number of transactions every day.

Step 3

After obtaining the IP address, the browser formed a connection to the server at that IP address on port 80. Any server machine makes its services available to the internet using numbered ports, one for each service that is available on the server. For example, if a server machine is running a web server and an FTP server, the web server would typically be available on port 80, and the FTP server would be available on port 21 (How ports work, n.d.).

Step 4

Following the hypertext transfer protocol, the browser sent a GET request to the server, asking for the file named **courses/buscomp**. At this stage, cookies may be sent from browser to server with the GET request. A cookie is a piece of text that a web server can store on a user's hard disk. Cookies allow a website to store information on a user's machine and later retrieve it. The pieces of information are stored as name-value pairs (Cookie basics, n.d.). Using cookies, sites can determine how many visitors arrive, how many are new (as opposed to repeat) visitors, how often a visitor has visited, and so on.

Step 5

The server then sent the HTML text for the web page to the browser.

Step 6

The browser read the HTML tags, formatted the page accordingly and displayed it on your screen.

What is HTML?

HTML (hypertext markup language) is the set of markup symbols or codes inserted in a file intended for display on a browser page. The markup tells the browser how to display a web page's text and images. Each individual markup code is referred to as an element (a tag). Some elements come in pairs that indicate when some display effect (such as italic text) is to begin and when it is to end. HTML is a formal recommendation by the World Wide Web Consortium (W3C) and is generally adhered to by the major browsers.

An HTML tag is a code element that will appear as letters or words between angled brackets:

> <title>, <body>

The end or closing tag is indicated by a forward slash:

> </title>, </body>

Most tags come in matched opening and closing pairs, but this is not an absolute rule. Any web page you create will contain the following tags at the start:

- **<HTML>**: this tells the browser that this is the beginning of an HTML document
- **<HEAD>**: this tells the browser that this is the header for the page
- **<TITLE>**: this tells the browser that this is the title of the page
- **<BODY>**: this tells the web browser that this is the beginning of the web page content – the rest of the page content follows this tag.

The tags needed to end any web page are:

- **</BODY>**
- **</HTML>**

You can create a web page by saving a document as an HTML file (i.e. with the extension **.htm** or **.html**). For example, the following text, saved as an HTML file, will display a web page in your browser as shown in Figure 1.1.

```
<html>
<head>
<title>My First Webpage</title>
</head>
<body>
<h1>
Hello there. Welcome to my web page.</h1>
</body>
</html>
```

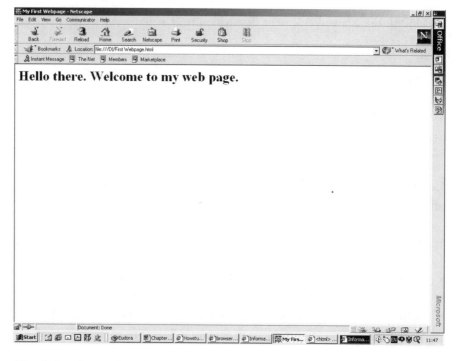

Fig. 1.1 *A sample web page*

Details of HTML codes and recent developments are available at the W3C web page (Hypertext markup language). However, in order to produce a web page, you need not necessarily learn and master HTML codes: various software packages are now available to help users create their own pages. These packages are similar to word-processing packages: users need only to specify the way they want a page to appear by using various format codes, links, etc., and the software creates the corresponding HTML codes behind the scene. Note that for a complete web page, the HTML codes may be quite long and complex. Figure 1.2 shows a simple web page, and Figure 1.3 shows the page containing the complicated HTML codes. Note that there is an option in the browser that allows users to view the HTML source for any page. Netscape Composer (part of the Netscape browser) and Microsoft FrontPage are examples of software that allows users to create web pages without the need to understand HTML. However, the more complicated the web page design, the more useful it is to learn and master the HTML codes.

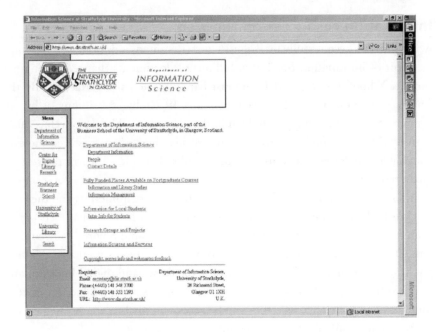

Fig. 1.2   *A simple web page*

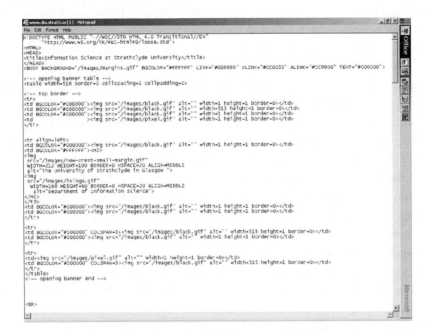

Fig. 1.3   *The HTML codes for the web page shown in Figure 1.2*

Information resources on the web

According to a recent study by BrightPlanet (Bergman, n.d.), the web is a huge reservoir of information filled with billions of documents that search engines such as Yahoo!, Google and Lycos just barely scratch the surface of. By the study's estimates, the 'surface web' contains 19 terabytes (trillions of bytes), compared with 7500 terabytes hidden in the 'deep web'. The deep web is qualitatively different from the surface web, because the content is stored there in searchable databases that only produce results dynamically in response to a direct request.

Information resources available through the web are numerous and they can be classified in a number of ways: from personal to institutional web pages; from research and academic information such as research reports, course materials, etc., to business information such as products, advertising materials; from publications such as books and journals to databases and digital libraries; and so on. While many of the web information resources are available free of cost, some have restricted access – they can be accessed only by certain categories of users – or are available upon payment.

The web technology is built on the rather simple idea of hypertext: if the information is not restricted, anyone can access a particular information resource simply by going to a web page through its URL, and from there follow the hyperlinks – within a particular page, to a particular site, or to other sites.

However, there is a problem. Imagine that you are searching for information in the world's largest library, which contains millions of documents, but those documents are not classified and catalogued. It is not true that web information resources are not at all organized: they are organized according to the IP address of the computer where they reside, and within a computer they can be identified by directory and file name. The problem is that there is no single catalogue, and the documents are not organized in the way we find them in a library.

What do we want to achieve when we search for information on the web? Simply speaking, we want to achieve effectiveness and efficiency. By effectiveness, we mean to get what is required (the information), and by efficiency we mean how fast and cheaply (in terms of search time, etc.) the required information is obtained. Therefore, in order to meet the effectiveness requirement, we need to know what is available where, and to attain efficiency we need to know how to pick up the right information item quickly and easily from among the millions available on the web. Keeping in mind the volume and variety of information available on the web, it is not always possible for someone to precisely know whether a particular piece of information is available, and if so where it is available. Fortunately, a large number of web search tools are freely available. These tools help us find out whether and where the information that we are looking for is available. We shall consider these tools in this book.

Information services on the web

Many new information services are now available through the web. The two most significant services that have made a tremendous impact on the information profession are the web-based reference and information services, and digital library services. These services now enable users to access digital information resources from their own computers. They also, in many cases, enable users to get answers to specific questions. We shall discuss some of these services with brief descriptions of their characteristics, etc. The immediacy and easy availability of these services are now setting a new trend in the information service sector, and this book ends with a brief note on this issue.

Chapter 2
Basic search techniques

Introduction

In order to retrieve information efficiently from the web, electronic journals or digital libraries, we need to use search tools. In this chapter we shall discuss the basic search techniques that the user needs to learn to be able to use search tools effectively. The exact search techniques and the corresponding search operators will depend on the search system chosen, and these will be discussed in subsequent chapters. We have discussed the basics of search techniques elsewhere (see, for example, Chowdhury, 1999a, and Chowdhury and Chowdhury, 2001), but their discussion here, with appropriate examples drawn from search engines, should serve as a helpful background to the rest of the book.

Word and phrase search

A search can be conducted by entering a single search term or a phrase comprising more than one term. The keyword search is the simplest form of search facility offered by a search system. Every search system – a search engine for the web or for a digital library – provides a search box where users type their search terms or phrase. The advanced search interfaces of web search engines provide facilities to make a search statement more specific. The following are examples of keyword and phrase search expressions using the *AltaVista* search engine:

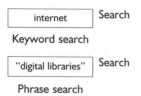

Most search engines allow searchers to enter a phrase within double quotes (see Table 3.1). In some cases, particularly in the advanced search interfaces of search engines, users are required to select radio buttons, or check boxes, for word or phrase searches. The terminologies used for word and phrase search may vary from one search engine to another. For example, in the FAST search engine, users are given three options to choose from: 'all of the words', 'any of the words' and 'the exact phrase'; in the HotBot search engine, the options are: 'all words', 'any word' and 'as a phrase'.

Boolean search

This is a very common search technique that combines search terms according to Boolean logic (Chowdhury, 1999a). Three types of Boolean search are possible: AND search, OR search and NOT search.

The AND search allows users to combine two or more search terms using the Boolean AND operator. The search will then retrieve those items that contain all the constituent terms. For example, the search expression 'Internet and libraries' will retrieve all those records where both the terms occur. Boolean AND search adds more restrictions to a search expression by adding more search terms. Therefore, the more search terms are ANDed, the more restricted, or specific, will be the search, and as a result the smaller will be the search output. A search may produce no results if too many search terms are ANDed.

The OR search allows users to combine two or more search terms, such that the system retrieves all those items that contain either one or all of the constituent terms. Thus, the search expression 'Internet or libraries' will retrieve all those records (1) where the term internet occurs, (2) where the term libraries occurs, and (3) where both the terms occur. Note that this is contrary to the use of the term 'or' in normal English. The OR search, though it adds more terms to a search expression, broadens rather than restricts a given expression, because the search is conducted for occurrences of each single ORed term, irrespective of whether any other term occurs. Consequently, the output of OR searches will be greater. When too many search terms are ORed, the search output may be too big to handle.

The NOT search allows users to specify those terms that they do not want to occur in the retrieved records. For example, the search expression 'search engines NOT AltaVista' will retrieve all the records on search engines except those where the term 'AltaVista' occurs. Boolean NOT searches restrict a search by forcing the search system to discard those items containing the NOT word(s). Hence, the search output will decrease with an increase in the NOT words.

Different approaches to conducting Boolean searches are taken in search engines. The most common approach is by combining the search terms using the Boolean AND, OR, NOT, or any corresponding operators. For example, in AltaVista and HotBot, Boolean searches can be conducted using Boolean AND, OR and AND NOT, and combining terms and operators using parentheses. However, most search engines use the plus and minus sign for Boolean AND and NOT searches. The plus operator (+) placed before a word or phrase means that all returned pages should contain that search term. Similarly the minus operator (–) can be placed before a word or phrase to exclude all documents containing that search term, and this implies the Boolean NOT search. In many search engines, users are required to select options from choices, such as: 'all the words', 'any of the words', etc. For example, in the FAST search engine users can choose the option 'all of the words' to imply the Boolean AND search, or 'any of the words' to imply the Boolean OR search; in HotBot the options are 'all words', and 'any word' for the Boolean AND and OR search respectively.

Truncation

Truncation is a search facility that enables a search to be conducted for all the different forms of a word having the same common root. As an example, the truncated word 'Librar*' will retrieve items containing the terms 'Library', 'Libraries', 'Librarian', etc. A number of different options are available for truncation, viz., right truncation, left truncation and masking of letters in the middle of the word. Left truncation retrieves all words having the same characters at the right-hand part, e.g. '*hyl' will retrieve words like 'methyl', 'ethyl', etc. Similarly, middle truncation retrieves all words having the same characters at the left and right hand part. For example, a middle-truncated search term 'colo*r' will retrieve both the terms 'colour' and 'color'. A wild card, such as '*' or '?' is used to allow any letter to appear in a specific location within a word.

Truncation as a search facility is supported by some search engines, not all. Right truncation and character masking or wild cards are the most common truncation search facilities available with search engines. However, the search operators and their applications vary. The following are some examples:

- in AltaVista, '*' is used for truncation; '*' stands for 0 to 5 characters
- in HotBot, '*' and '?' are used for truncation; '*' is used for 0 or more char-

acters, while '?' is used to replace only one character

- in Northern Light, '*' and '%' are used for truncation; '*' is used to replace multiple characters, while '%' is used for only one character.

In some search engines, for example in MSN, users can activate stemming (which works like right truncation in the sense that variant forms of the search term, having the same root, are searched) simply by choosing the option 'enable stemming'.

Proximity search

This search facility allows users to specify the distance between two search terms in the retrieved results. The proximity search is similar, in principle, to the Boolean AND search, except that it makes the search more restricted. Therefore, proximity searches are likely to produce more specific results compared with a simple Boolean AND search. Search engines that support proximity searching vary significantly in terms of operators and their implementation. For example:

- in AltaVista, the operator NEAR is used between two search terms to indicate that the specified search terms should occur at the most ten words apart from one another
- in Lycos, the operator ADJ is used to indicate that two search terms should appear next to each other; the NEAR operator followed by a number indicates how many words the search terms may be apart at the most (the maximum number is 25); FAR is used to denote that two search terms should occur 25 words or more apart.

Field or meta tag search

A searcher may sometimes want to restrict a search to a specific field with a view to obtaining more specific results. Searchers can specify the field tag by selecting an appropriate option, provided by a search engine, or by typing the field name before the search term(s). In the search engine terminology this is called a meta tag search, since the fields in the web pages are specified by meta tags. Search engines allow users to restrict a search to a meta tag by preceding a search term or phrase with an appropriate meta tag and a colon. In AltaVista a search can be restricted to a number of meta tags by specifying the tag followed by a colon and the search term(s), e.g. title: "Ministry of Education"; domain:

edu, and so on. Similar meta tag search facilities are available in other search engines, such as Excite, Infoseek, HotBot, and so on. In some search engines, searchers can restrict a search to a specific field or meta tag by choosing the appropriate option. For example, in FAST a searcher can specify whether the search term(s) should appear in the text, title, link or URL simply by checking the appropriate box in the advanced search screen.

Limiting search

Sometimes users may want to limit a given search by using certain criteria, such as language, year of publication, type of information sources, and so on. These are called limiting searches. This is particularly useful in the web environment, where a simple search can produce millions of hits. Criteria that can be used in a limiting search depend on the chosen search engine:

- in AltaVista users can limit a search by language and date
- in Excite a search can be limited by language, domain and country
- in HotBot a search can be limited by language, date (within the last week, last two weeks, month, three months, year, etc.) and search sites.

Usually search engines provide the options in boxes or as radio buttons for searchers to select the appropriate limiting criteria.

Summary

In this chapter we discussed the basic techniques used for conducting an information search using a search engine. There are common search techniques that are available in many search engines. Just as every search technique discussed here is not available in every search engine, some search engines have some unique search facilities. These are discussed along with some selected search engines in Chapter 3. Features of some search systems used for searching electronic journals and digital libraries are discussed in Chapters 7 and 8 respectively.

Chapter 3
Search engines

Introduction

There are basically two ways to search the web: by conducting a search using a search engine, or by following the links in a specially designed list called a directory (discussed in Chapter 4). Search engines allow the user to enter search terms – keywords and/or phrases – that are run against a database containing information on the web pages collected automatically by programs called spiders. The search engine retrieves web pages from its database that match the search terms entered by the searcher. It is important to note that when a user conducts a search using a search engine, the latter does not search for the information across the entire web at the given instance. Instead, it searches a fixed database, located at the search engine's website containing information on selected web pages. It is updated at regular intervals according to the specific criteria employed by the search engine.

While all search engines are intended to perform the same task, each goes about doing so in a different way, and this sometimes causes wildly different results. Factors that influence the search results include the size of the database, frequency of updating, criteria employed for indexing the chosen web pages, and the search capabilities. Search engines also differ in their search speed, the design of the search interface, the way in which they display the search results, the amount of help available, and so on.

How do search engines work?

Search engines run from special sites on the web and are designed to help people find information stored on other sites. There are differences in the ways the various search engines work, but they all perform the following three basic tasks:

- they search the internet – or select parts of the internet – based on a set of criteria.
- they keep an index of the words/phrases they find, with specific information such as where they found them, how many times they found them, etc.
- they allow users to search for words/phrases or combinations of words/phrases found in that index.

There are three main components of a search engine: the spider, the index, and the search engine software and interface.

The spider

To find information on the millions of web pages that exist, a search engine employs a special program, called a spider, to build lists of the terms found on websites. A spider automatically fetches web pages for search engines; it is called a spider because it crawls over the web (*Webopedia* website). Web pages contain links to other pages, and a spider uses these links. As soon as it sees a link to another page, it visits the page, reads it, and then follows links to other pages within the site. The spider returns to the site on a regular basis, such as every week or month, to look for changes. The usual starting points are lists of heavily used servers and very popular pages. The spider will begin with a popular site, indexing the words on its pages and following every link found within the site. In this way, the spidering system quickly begins to travel, spreading out across the most widely used portions of the web. Figure 3.1 shows the process of web indexing in a simplified form.

Spiders select words occurring in the title, subtitles, meta tags and other positions of relative importance on selected web pages. The selection criteria vary from one spider to another, and these different approaches usually result in the differences in the search results. For example, some spiders keep track of the words in the title, subheadings and links, along with the most frequently used words on the page and each word in the first few lines of text, and so on. Lycos is said to use this approach to spidering the web, while others, such as AltaVista, go in the other direction, indexing every single word on a page (How Internet search engines work, n.d.). Meta tags play an important role in the search process: through these the owner of a page can specify the keywords and con-

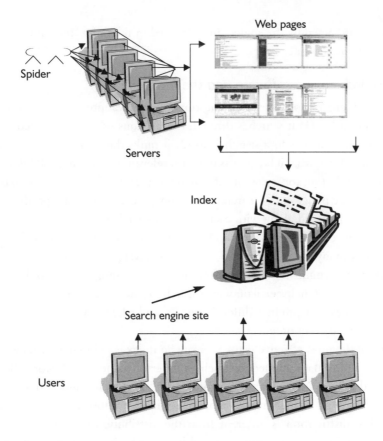

Fig. 3.1   *The process of web indexing and searching*

cepts under which the page should be indexed. However, not all search engines give the same importance to meta tags. For example, HotBot and InfoSeek accord greater importance to pages with keywords in their meta tags, but Excite does not (Search engine resources, n.d.).

The index

All the terms that a spider finds go into the index. If the content of a web page changes, then the spider notices it, brings back the new information and thus updates the index with the new information. However, it may take a while before the changes in a web page are found and indexed by a search engine, depending on several factors, such as how frequently the spider visits the same pages, how frequently the index is updated and so on. Until the changes in a web page are noted by the spider, and included in the index, they are not considered by the search engine.

The search engine software and the interface

The search engine software is the information retrieval program that performs two major tasks: (1) it searches through the millions of terms recorded in the index to find matches to a search, and (2) it ranks the retrieved records (web pages) in order of what it believes is the most relevant (Chowdhury, 1999a). The criteria for selection (or rejection) of search terms and assigning weight to them depend on the policy of the search engine concerned, as does the specific information that is stored along with each keyword – such as where in a given web page it occurred (in the heading, in links, in the meta tags or in the title of the page), how many times it occurred, the attached weight, and so on. Each commercial search engine has a different formula for assigning weight to the words in its index, which helps explain why a search for the same word using different search engines may produce different results, and why the web pages retrieved may be in a different order.

One of the most effective ways to create an index is to build a hash table. In hashing, a formula is applied to attach a numerical value to each word (Baeza-Yates and Ribeiro-Neto, 1999; Chowdhury, 1999a). The formula is designed to evenly distribute entries across a predetermined number of divisions. This numerical distribution is different from the distribution of words across the alphabet, and that is the strength of hashing. The basic idea is to convert a key – a word, a number, etc. – into a number that can directly specify where in the memory the key should be placed. Users looking for a particular key can be directed to the specific memory location where the key is stored. It is like a hotel register that stores the room number against the name of each of its guests. Users search the index through a query. A query can be as simple as a single word, or more complex, comprising several words and/or phrases interposed with various search operators. The combination of efficient indexing and effective storage makes it possible to get results quickly, even for complex search queries.

Types of search engine

The results of a web search largely depend on the chosen search engine, because search engines differ in the way they select, update and index information, as well as the search and retrieval features that they offer (Glossbrenner and Glossbrenner, 1999; Poulter, Tseng and Sargent, 1999). Search engines can be categorized in a number of ways. Two broad categories are search engines and meta search engines, the latter referring to tools that allow users to conduct concurrent searches on more than one search engine. Search engines can also be categorized on the basis of their indexing characteristics. For example, Nicholson (1998) categorizes search engines as full-text search tools, extracting search tools, subject-specific search tools and meta search tools. Sullivan (n.d.) of Searchenginewatch.com lists the following eight categories of search engines:

- major search engines, such as, AltaVista, Excite, FAST Search
- news search engines, such as Moreover, NewsIndex, InfoGrid
- specialty search engines, such as Ask Jeeves, Web Help
- kids search engines, such as AOL Kids Only, KidsClick, Yahooligans
- metacrawlers, such as Dogpile, Metacrawler, Cnet Search
- multimedia search engines, such as MP3.com, Audiogalaxy
- regional search engines, such as Mosaique, Indiainfo.com, Japanese search engines
- search utilities, such as Copernic, InfoSeek Express, Lexibot.

Features of selected search engines

In this section we shall discuss the features of selected search engines with a view to finding out their common search and retrieval capabilities. We shall also highlight the special features of each search engine. Originally search engines were devised as a tool for providing users with a search interface that could be used to search the web, as opposed to the directories that were designed to provide various search categories that could be browsed by users to select a particular website. However, search engines have also begun to provide browsable directories as part of their search interfaces, thereby giving users options to search or browse. Figure 3.2 shows the first page of AltaVista, which offers search facilities and directories on the same screen; the Google home page (Figure 3.3) has a link to its directory; FAST Search (Figure 3.4) has no directory. Nevertheless, search engines are still characterized by the automatic selection and indexing of web pages, as opposed to directories, which are not indexed but are placed in a particular category based on its subject and/or contents. Table 3.1 provides a quick overview of the essential features of ten search engines.

Fig. 3.2 *AltaVista home page*

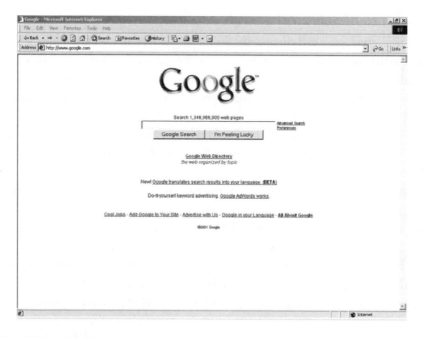

Fig. 3.3 *Google home page*

Fig. 3.4 *FAST Search home page*

Table 3.1 *Essential features of ten search engines*

Search engine	Features
AltaVista	• Word, phrase and natural language search facilities are available.
	• Simple and advanced search options are available.
	• Special search for image, audio and video is possible.
	• A number of categories are available for browsing.
	• It supports multilingual search.
	• Users can search a specific language.
	• Boolean search: AND, OR, AND NOT; + and − signs are used to indicate that the following search term must or must not appear; Parentheses can be used for nested Boolean search. In the advanced search mode, there are three options, and one can be chosen after entering a word/phrase: Must Have, Good to Have and Must Not Have.
	• Proximity search: NEAR Finds documents containing both specified words or phrases within 10 words of each other.

(continued)

Table 3.1 *(continued)*

Search engine	Features
	• Truncation: * is used as a truncation operator which stands for 0-5 characters, and can be used only after 3 characters.
	• Phrase search: A phrase is to be entered within double quotes.
	• Meta tag search: Possible on Anchor, applet, domain, host, image, like, link, text, title and URL.
	• Searches can be limited by language and date.
	• Ranking: Result pages are considered more relevant if they have (1) more instances of the search terms, (2) search terms that are preceded by + in the query, (3) search terms that appear in relatively few other pages, or (4) search terms that are closer together in the text. Pages that have the opposite qualities are considered less relevant.
	• Sorting: In the advanced search, there is no automatic ranking. Users can control the ranking of results by entering the words that they want them sorted by in the 'Sort by' box. If 'Sort by' box is left blank, the results appear in random order.
	• Link: The keyword 'link:', followed by a domain name or a complete URL, returns every web page that has a hypertext link to a particular site, directory, or page.
	• Translate: Automatic translation of web pages from selected languages is available.
	• Family filter: Can be turned on or off to allow/avoid retrieval of unwanted materials.
AOL Search	• Word, phrase and natural language queries.
	• Simple and advanced search options are available.
	• Special search for news, photo and audio search facilities are available.
	• A number of categories are available for browsing.
	• Users can decide to search AOL and the web, AOL only, or web only.

(continued)

Table 3.1 *(continued)*

Search engine	Features

- Boolean search: AND, OR, AND NOT; + and – signs are used to indicate that the following search term must or must not appear; Parentheses can be used for nested Boolean search. AOL Search assumes an AND between words, but even if the user uses ORs and retrieves a large number of documents, the ones near the top of the list will tend to be the same documents they would have retrieved with AND. In the advanced search mode users can select the options like 'All of the words', 'Any of the words', and 'Must contain', or 'Must not contain'.
- Phrase search: A phrase is to be entered within double quotes.
- Truncation: '?' is used to replace one character and '*' is used for wild card; '!' is used as a concept operator: a search for the word accidents! finds documents on the subject of accidents, even if they don't contain the word 'accident'.
- Proximity search: three operators are available, viz. ADJ, W/n, and NEAR/n.
- Searches can be limited by language, domain and country.

Excite
- Word, phrase and natural language queries.
- Simple and advanced search options are available.
- Special search for news, photo and audio search facilities are available.
- A number of categories are available for browsing.
- Supports multilingual search. Users can search a specific language.
- Boolean search: AND, OR, AND NOT; + and – signs are used to indicate that the search term following must or must not appear; parentheses can be used for nested Boolean search.
- Phrase search: A phrase is to be entered within double quotes.
- Searches can be limited by language, domain and country.

(continued)

Table 3.1 *(continued)*

Search engine	Features
	• Ranking is based on the content of the web pages, their meta-tags, referring anchor text, and link popularity. • If the 'View by URL' option is chosen, the output list will compress to display website titles and relevant documents contained within the sites. • The 'Show summaries' option displays the site summaries of search results.
FAST	• Simple and advanced search facilities are available. • Word and phrase search options are available. • A separate multimedia search facility is available. • Does not have any directories to browse. • It supports multilingual search. Users can search a specific language. Users can customize the interface to suit a chosen language. • Boolean search: + and – signs are used to indicate that the search term following must or must not appear. Terms entered within parentheses without being separated by any operator are considered to be connected by OR. In the simple search one can choose any of the three options: all of the words, any of the words, the exact phrase. • In the advanced search, a sequence of entered words is considered as a phrase. • Searchers can specify that a word/phrase should appear in the text, title, link, URL or link to the URL. • Searches can be limited by language, and domain (top level domain like 'edu', 'gov', etc.). • Offensive content reduction option can be made on or off to allow/avoid retrieval of offensive materials.
Google	• Word and phrase search facilities are available. • Simple and advanced search options are available. • A separate link for *Google Directory* gives access to several browsable categories.

(continued)

Table 3.1 *(continued)*

Search engine	Features
	• It supports multilingual search. Users can search in a specific language.
	• Boolean search: Two or more search terms are automatically ANDed; OR is used to join search terms by the OR operator; '-' sign is used to indicate that the term following should not occur.
	• Phrase search: A phrase has to be entered within double quotes.
	• Searches can be limited by language, link and site; it also allows to find pages that are related to a given web page.
	• Stop words: Searchers can use the '+' sign to include stop words in their search.
	• I'm Feeling Lucky Option: This option automatically takes the searcher directly to the first web page *Google* returned for a query.
	• Statistics bar: This line describes the search and indicates the number of results returned as well as the amount of time it took to complete the search.
	• It ranks pages according to relevance, number of times sites are visited, etc.
	• Google search facilities can easily be added to the user's web browser.
	• It makes suggestions should spelling mistakes occur.
HotBot	• Quick, advanced, multimedia, and directory search facilities are available.
	• Words and phrase search options are available.
	• A number of categories are available for browsing.
	• It supports multilingual search. Users can search in a specific language.
	• Boolean search: AND, OR, AND NOT operators can be used; '+' and '-' signs are used to indicate whether the following search term must or must not appear; users can

(continued)

Table 3.1 *(continued)*

Search engine	Features
	select the 'All words' option for the Boolean AND, or 'Any word' option for Boolean OR. Three choices are available in the simple search: 'All words', 'Any word' or 'As a phrase'.

- Truncation: Word stemming option can be activated in the advanced search mode.* (asterisk): matches 0 or more characters; ? (question mark): matches exactly one character.
- Phrase search: phrases are to be entered within double quotes.
- Searches can be conducted on a number of meta tags.
- Searches can be limited by language, date (last week, 2 weeks, month, 3 months, year, etc.), and search sites.
- Searchers can specify whether a page must have a video, audio, PDF file, etc. Searchers can choose the option: 'must contain', 'should contain', 'must not contain'.
- The family filter option can be turned on to avoid the retrieval of offensive materials.
- Sorting: Search results can be sorted by relevance, size, URL or date.
- Page links analyser allows the user to search for documents that contain hyperlinks to a designated web document.
- Special commands: Some special commands can be used to look for special types of materials on the pages, e.g. feature:applet detects embedded Java applets; feature:image detects image files (GIF, JPEG, etc.), and so on. Some special commands can be used to restrict the search, e.g. domain:[name] restricts a search to the domain selected; link:[url] lets you identify the number of documents that link to a specific document (exact URL).

Magellan
- Simple and advanced search options are available.
- A number of categories are available for browsing.
- The Find Similar button next to the title tells Magellan to use that document as an example in a new search.

(continued)

Table 3.1 *(continued)*

Search engine	Features
	• AND, OR, AND NOT; + and − signs are used to indicate that the search term following must or must not appear; Parentheses can be used for nested Boolean search. • Phrase search: phrases are to be entered within double quotes.
MSN	• Simple and advanced search facilities are available. • A number of categories are available for browsing. • Boolean search: the operators are AND, NOT and AND NOT (all in capitals); + and − signs are used to indicate that the search term following must or must not appear. • Truncation: Asterisk '*' may be used as a wild card for truncation; users can select an option to enable stemming to activate truncation. • Users can select the options: any of the words, all of the words, words in the title, the exact phrase, Boolean phrase, or links to the URL. • Searches can also be limited by region, language, date and domain. • Users can specify whether results should contain multimedia information such as image, audio, video, etc. • Allows users to change the content, layout and colour of the page.
Northern Light	• Word, phrase and natural language search facilities are available. • Simple search, power (advanced) search, business search, Investext search and stock search facilities are available. • There is no specific directory for users to browse. • Quotes search, current news search and Geo search options are available. • Various search options, e.g. search for company name, publishers, Investment text, Geo text, etc. are available. • Boolean search: AND, OR, AND NOT; + and − signs are

(continued)

Table 3.1 (*continued*)

Search engine	Features
	used to indicate that the following search term must or must not appear.
	• Truncation: the * (asterisk) is used to replace multiple characters, and the % symbol is used to replace only one character.
	• Phrase search: phrases are to be entered within double quotes.
	• Field/meta tag searches can be conducted by URL, title, text, publisher, company, Ticker (company's stock ticker), and RECID (Northern Light Special Collection number).
	• Limiting search: Searches can be limited by subject, type of document, site or date
	• Sorting: Results can be sorted by relevance or date/time.
Web Crawler	• Words, phrase and natural language search facilities are available.
	• A number of categories are available for browsing.
	• Boolean search: the operators are AND, OR, NOT ; + and – signs are used to indicate that the search term following must or must not appear; Parentheses can be used for nested Boolean search.
	• Phrase search: phrases are to be entered within double quotes.

Meta search engines

One of the major problems of the web is that it is too big and growing too fast to be covered and indexed comprehensively by any one search engine. Major search engines can cover and index only a small fraction of the entire web. As a result, when a user searches the web using a particular search engine, he/she may not find a particular piece of information simply because the relevant page was not covered or indexed properly by the search engine. The user can of course repeat his or her search using different search engines, but this is time-consuming. To avoid this inconvenience, meta search engines have been devised, which allow users to conduct searches concurrently on a number of search engines. Some meta search engines conduct searches with a fixed set of search engines, while others allow users to choose which search engines to use. For example, the meta search engine Dogpile searches three search engines at a time. If the searcher does not get at least ten documents matching the query from the displayed results, Dogpile will automatically search the next three engines. The process will continue until all the search engines are used or ten matches are found. If more than ten results are found, the searcher can simply press the 'Next' button to get results from the next three search engines. If a particular search engine finds more than ten results, there will be a link to search the next set of results. Users can customize a search to change the order in which the engines are searched. Table 3.2 lists the essential features of three meta search engines.

Special search engines

Because there are millions of items available on the web, and a given search can produce a huge number of items, or hits, search engines are making constant efforts to produce better and more relevant results. Some of this research involves using statistical analysis on pages containing the words or phrases searched for, in order to find those pages that may be of interest to the searcher. Obviously, to accomplish this, a search engine has to store a lot of information about each page it indexes, and consequently more processing is required for each search.

An important feature of many search engines is that they do not always require users to enter complex search expressions using complex search operators. While some search engines allow users to enter natural language queries, most allow users to choose options that are clearly laid out as radio buttons or search option boxes. Thus, in most cases searchers may just click on a button or a box to specify whether to search for any or all the words that have been entered, whether to search the entered words as a phrase, whether to limit the search within a specific field, and so on. This has significantly reduced the complexities of traditional information retrieval facilities. However, the idea behind natural language queries is that users can type a question in the same way they would ask a human, and therefore they don't need to keep track of Boolean or other search operators or complex query structures.

Table 3.2 *Essential features of three meta search engines*

Meta search engine	Features
Dogpile	• Word and phrase search facilities are available
	• Boolean Search: the operators are AND, OR, NOT; + and – are used to indicate that the following search term must/must not appear
	• Users can choose to search the web (using AltaVista, Direct Hit, Dogpile Web Catalog, FindWhat, Google, GoTo.com, InfoSeek, Kanoodle, LookSmart, Lycos, Open Directory, RealNames and Yahoo!); images (using Ditto.com); audio/MP3 (using Astraweb, AudioGalaxy, MP3Board); auctions (using GoTo.com); news (using Thunderstone); FTP (using Fast FTP Search); discussion (Usenet) (using Deja.com and Deja.com's old database); and multimedia (using Singingfish.com)
	• It searches 3 search engines at a time; if at least 10 documents are not found, another 3 search engines are automatically searched.
Intelliseek	• Simple, all, any, Boolean and phrase search options are available: 'All' or 'Any' options (equivalent to Boolean AND and OR simultaneously) can be chosen, and Boolean AND (or &), OR (or |) and NOT (or !) can be used
	• Users can choose the best 3, fastest 3, all or any of the 9 search tools, viz. About, AltaVista, Britannica, Direct Hit, Excite, Go, Look Smart, Lycos, Yahoo!.
Mamma	• 'Phrase', 'and', or 'or' options can be chosen in the advanced search interface
	• It sends queries to 8 search engines (Yahoo!, Lycos, Ask Jeeves, FindWhat, InfoSeek, Go To, MSN and NBCi), creates a virtual database, organizes the results into a uniform format and presents them by relevance and source

(continued)

Table 3.2 *(continued)*

Meta search engine	Features
	• Users can choose to search for the web, news, audio, video or MP3
	• Adult filters may turned on or off
	• Users can choose to set the number of results per page
	• Users can set time for time out (5, 10, 15, 30, 60 seconds or 2 minutes)

One of the most popular natural language query sites is Ask Jeeves. Users can ask a simple question and Jeeves comes up with answers and/or a set of related questions, and/or hits from other search tools such as AltaVista, Yahoo!, etc. One of the unique features of Ask Jeeves is that it can take the user to the page containing the answer to his/her query. It opens the relevant page, and on top an Ask Jeeves frame appears that allows the user to print the answer, modify the query, and so on.

Another unique feature of Ask Jeeves is that in addition to the results from various search engines, it comes up with a number of predefined queries related to the question that has been asked. Many of these predefined questions come up with small boxes with a list of queries, and the searcher can click on the 'Ask' button to put any one of these to Ask Jeeves as a query (see, for example, Figure 3.5). Ask Jeeves also has a list of popular questions, and users can click on any one of them to put it to Ask Jeeves as a query. Ask Jeeves processes and categorizes all the queries that it receives, and presents related questions on the screen when a question is asked by a user. In most cases, unlike most other search or meta search engines, Ask Jeeves takes the user to the appropriate website that contains the answer (see Figure 3.6).

Summary

As shown in Tables 3.1 and 3. 2, search engines and meta search engines differ in terms of the search and retrieval facilities that they offer. Some search engines have more sophisticated search features than others. Many search engines provide separate search facilities for multimedia documents – audio, video, etc. Some search engines, such as Ask Jeeves, have special features that allow the user to formulate a query in a natural way, or to get an answer to a query that has been preformulated by search engine experts.

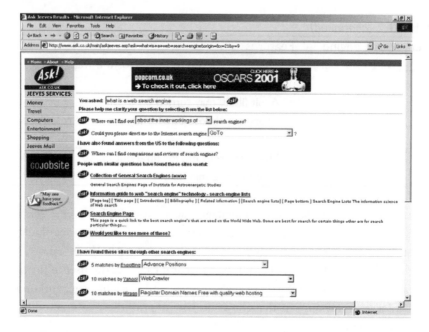

Fig. 3.5 *Ask Jeeves page showing various query frames*

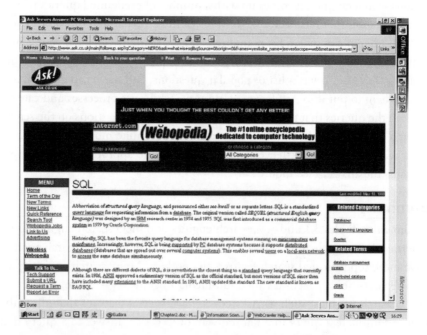

Fig 3.6 *Ask Jeeves provides the answer to the query 'What is SQL?'*

It may be difficult for novice users to know which particular search engine to use. Many suggestions and tips for conducting useful web searches are available in the literature (see, for example, Clarke, 1998; Hume, 2000; Sullivan, n.d.; Tyner, n.d., which can be summarized as follows:

- when you find a useful site, bookmark it
- basic knowledge of the way in which URLs are constructed will help you to guess the correct URL for a given website
- often a search will retrieve links to many documents at one site; rather than clicking on each URL in succession to find the desired document, truncate the URL at the point at which it appears most likely to represent the document you are seeking, and type this URL in the location box of your web browser
- it is better to do many narrow searches than to make a search that is too broad
- use Boolean AND and phrase options whenever possible to make a search more specific
- use subject-specific search engines to give more specific results
- for comprehensive coverage use a meta search engine
- some search engines are case-sensitive, so use lower-case letters
- put the most important word first in your query
- while looking for names or something specific, use the exact phrase option.

Search engines are the most fascinating information retrieval tools that are available today free of charge. They are constantly improving their web search facilities. The latest information about search engines can be obtained from their websites (see the list of sites in the References, p. 164). There are also a number of printed and online sources that provide updates on various search engines and information on their comparative features, and so on: see, for example, Sonnenreich and Macinta, 1998; Hock, 1998,1999; Courtois and Michael, 1999; Notess, 1999; Sherman, 1999; Green, 2000; Sullivan, 2000, and the Nielsen NetRatings and Location Power websites.

Chapter 4
Web directories

Introduction

Directories are usually human-compiled guides to the web. They contain various categories and subcategories for organizing websites according to their contents. Users need to select a particular category in order to find web pages containing the required information. Although web search engines and directories are both used for finding information on the web, they find, store and present the information differently. One key difference between a search engine and a web directory is that a directory has a structure: it aims to organize web information resources in a hierarchy that can be browsed, whereas a search engine creates an index of terms extracted from web pages, and users are required to search the index to find web pages matching the search term(s) or phrase(s).

Figure 4.1 shows the various categories and subcategories in the Yahoo! directory. As shown in the figure, a searcher looking for information on digital libraries can choose the main category Reference, which leads to a subdirectory containing an entry for Libraries, which contains another subdirectory for Digital Libraries. The hierarchy of subdirectories continues until there are none left, at which stage the web pages on the chosen topic are listed.

A searcher using a search engine rather than a directory would enter the phrase 'digital libraries' in the search box, and the search engine would come up with a list of relevant web pages. The searcher would need to consider how to enter the phrase, whether to use a singular or plural for library, and so on. The output list would contain far too many results (though they may be sorted by usefulness) compared with the directory search results. Thus, in a directory search users need not worry about selecting the exact search terms, and need not

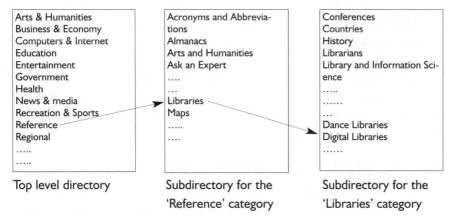

| Top level directory | Subdirectory for the 'Reference' category | Subdirectory for the 'Libraries' category |

Fig. 4.1   *Categories and subcategories in Yahoo!*

learn complex search techniques. All that a searcher needs is to select an appropriate category and follow the subcategories.

Directories and search engines have different approaches to the way they organize and present information. For example, the Yahoo! directory is built by editors – humans who decide where to list each site within the subject-based structure. Yahoo! editors do not include every page of every site on the entire web; they place the main page of any given site into an appropriate, subject-based category. Contrarily, search engines run automated programs that continually scan the web's vast content, page by page, storing all, or much, of the information found along the way. However, although web directories aim to organize web information resources in hierarchically organized categories, and expect users to browse categories to find the required information, they also provide search facilities.

Because of the different approaches to storing and presenting web content, directories and search engines have different uses. If the searcher is looking for a broad list of sites on the same subject, they should use a directory. If the searcher is looking for a very specific page within a site, they should try a search engine. By analogy with the book, the contents page can be considered as a directory, and the index as the index file that the search engine consults.

There are difficulties associated with directories, such as the need for correct mapping of the user query onto an appropriate category. If a searcher cannot select the most appropriate category from the first page (the top-level directory), then there is little chance that he/she will get into the right subdirectory. Other problems are caused by cross-classification of web pages by directories, and so on.

The features of the web directories discussed below will give a general idea of the nature and characteristics of web search directories. However, like search engines, web directories are also constantly evolving and are improving their features. The latest information about a directory may be obtained from its web page, as well as from printed and online resources (see, for example, Sullivan, n.d.; Tyner, n.d.; Glossbrenner and Glossbrenner, 1999; and the Location Power and Nielsen Netratings websites).

Features of selected web directories

In this section we shall discuss the features of five web directories, including their search facilities. Three of these – Yahoo!, Lycos and LookSmart – are quite large directories, while the other two – Argus Clearinghouse and the WWW Virtual Library – are much smaller, but we have chosen them for specific reasons. Argus Clearinghouse originated at the School of Information at the University of Michigan: its staff is made up of 'dedicated individuals who either have or are studying for Master's Degrees in Information and Library Science' (Argus Clearinghouse web page), and thus it is designed and managed by information science professionals. The WWW Virtual Library is a distributed, not-for-profit system comprising specialized directories and guides, each maintained by an expert in the field. Thus, the content of each site is solely the responsibility of the maintainer of that site.

Yahoo!

The Yahoo! directory is created by human editors who visit and evaluate websites, and then organize them into subject-based categories and subcategories. All of the site listings in the directory are placed within the main categories that appear on the Yahoo! home page (Figure 4.2). These categories are: Arts & Humanities, Business & Economy, Computers & Internet, Education, Entertainment, Government, Health, News & Media, Recreation & Sports, Reference, Regional, Science, Social Science, and Society & Culture.

Here is an example of a web search using the Yahoo! directory. We wanted to find information on metadata, and took the following path:

Home >> Reference (Libraries) >> Digital Libraries >> Metadata

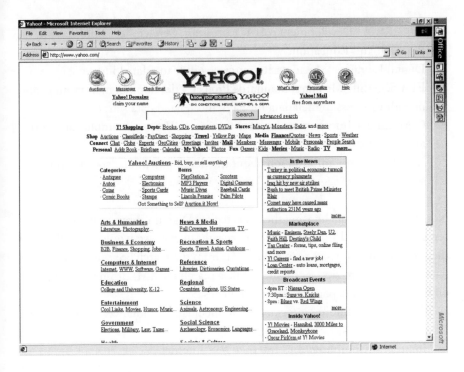

Fig. 4.2   *Yahoo! home page*

We were then shown a list of categories (each of which is hyperlinked) comprising sites under eight headings:

- Biological@
- Dublin Core
- Encoded Archival Description (EAD)
- Geospatial@
- Meta Content Framework (MCF)
- Platform for Internet Content Selection (PICS)
- ROADS
- URIs – Universal Resource Identifiers

Below the list of categories was a list of sites with brief information. Each of these sites is hyperlinked, and a click on any one would have taken us to a relevant page. Some of these sites were:

- DESIRE – Development of a European Service for Information on Research and Education.
- Digital Libraries: Metadata Resources – guide to related links.
- EPA Scientific Metadata Standards Project – developing, maintaining, and providing access to metadata for EPA and related data sets.
- Government Information Locator Service (GILS) – a sampler of information locators.
- IMS Metadata – information about the development of a specification and software for managing online learning resources.

Note that, instead of choosing the subcategory Digital Libraries, if we had chosen the Library and Information Science subcategory we would have obtained the same sets of results. A search for XML from the search box within the Metadata subcategory retrieved one site, while a search for XML from the search box on the Yahoo! home page found 162 matches.

With a view to finding information on metadata, we followed another route:

Home >> Computers and Internet >> Internet

There was no Metadata subcategory, though there are related subcategories such as HTML, XML, VRML, etc. We then searched for metadata in the search box, selecting 'just this category', and got three matches, though they were not as useful as the previous search results. This shows that it is extremely important to map a query correctly onto the categories proposed by the web directory.

Yahoo! search

As shown in Figure 4.2, instead of browsing the Yahoo! categories, you can conduct a search by entering a search term/phrase in the search box. Search facilities are also available on other pages. A user can go to any subdirectory and can conduct a search within that subdirectory. A Yahoo! search looks for matches with: category names, website titles and comments (as they appear in the Yahoo! directory), content from individual web pages (a service provided by Google, Yahoo! news stories, and Yahoo! net events. The search results are presented in that same order.

In Yahoo! search, a phrase has to be entered within double quotes. A '+' sign preceding a search term/phrase ensures it appears in the results; similarly, a '-' sign excludes it.

Browsing the Yahoo! directory is particularly useful for novice users, and for those who are not experts in the subject they are searching. It is also very good for broad searches, but if specific information on a topic is required, then a Yahoo! search is a better choice. A searcher can restrict a search within a particular Yahoo! subdirectory, or can search the entire Yahoo! site.

Lycos

Like Yahoo!, Lycos is a web directory providing access to categorized web information resources. The main Lycos categories are shown in Figure 4.3. Lycos also provides a search box that can be used to conduct a word/phrase search.

We wanted to look for information on metadata using the Lycos directory. We went through the following path: Home >> Computers >> Internet, but could not find a Metadata subcategory. We then searched for 'metadata' within the Computers category, but were unsuccessful. We went back to the Lycos home page and conducted the search there, and this time we got many relevant web pages. At this stage Lycos suggested that 'people who searched for this also

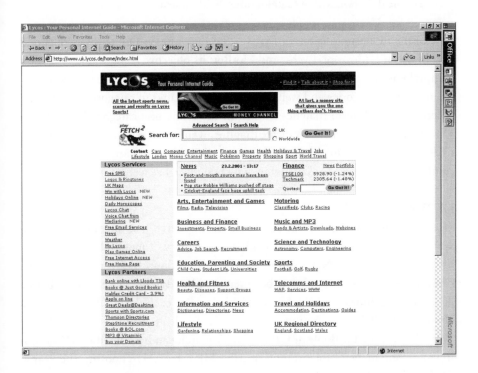

Fig. 4.3   *Lycos home page*

searched for Repository', which provided us with a new search term. By looking at the results, we noted that the Lycos directory path to metadata is:

> Reference >> Libraries >> Library and Information Science >>
> Technical Services >> Cataloguing >> Metadata

We went back to the Lycos home page, and took the following path: Reference >> Libraries >> Digital Libraries, which led to a list of sites on digital libraries, at the bottom of which was the following:

- Reference >> Bibliography >> Digital_Resources (3)
- Business >> Industries >> Publishing >> Publishers >> Electronic (119)
- Computers >> Software >> Information_Retrieval (144)
- Reference >> Knowledge_Management (586)
- Reference >> Libraries >> Library_and_Information_Science >> Technical_Services >> Cataloguing > Metadata

One of the interesting featureof Lycos is the Lycos Open Directory, a collaboration between DMoz.org, Lycos, and HotBot: its objective is to produce the most comprehensive taxonomy of web content. When a search is conducted on Lycos, often a list of categories and websites is displayed. Links to categories will appear where the search term matches a word in the name of a category in the Open Directory. Links to websites indicate that the given search term appears in the title or description of an Open Directory listing. All of these links are ranked above the results from the Lycos search engine, which are listed as web pages.

Lycos search

Users can enter a search term or phrase in the search box to conduct a Lycos search. The search can also be specific to a category of materials, for example, the fast-breaking Top News stories, the Pictures & Sounds directory, and so on. A phrase in a Lycos search has to be entered within double quotes, and as before a '+' sign includes a term/phrase, and a '-' sign excludes it. A searcher can choose the 'All Words' option to conduct a Boolean AND search, and 'Any Words' to conduct a Boolean OR search. A search can be refined by (1) choosing the content type, for example music, MP3, etc.; (2) choosing the search fields, title, URL and/or host/domain; or (3) by choosing a specific language.

LookSmart

LookSmart is another large and frequently used web directory. It categorizes web resources into hierarchies for browsing by users, and also provides search facilities. Figure 4.4 shows the LookSmart home page.

Users can browse through categories or topics. Once again we wanted to look for information on metadata, and took the following path, without finding any suitable subcategory:

> Home >> Library >> Reference >> Libraries & Archives >> Library
> Science

The subcategories of the Library Science category were:

- Guides & Directories
- Associations
- Library Fun & Humor
- Journals
- Library Schools
- Professional Development
- Topics.

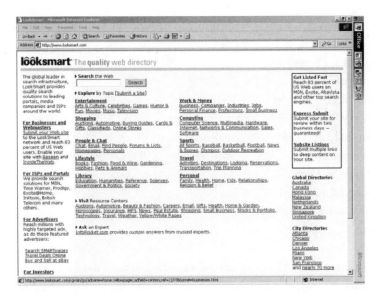

Fig 4.4   *LookSmart home page*

Since we could not find any information on metadata through the LookSmart categories, we entered the term in the search box, which obtained a number of results. In another search we were looking for XML, and took the following path:

Home>> Computing >> Internet >> Internet Industry >> Policies & Standards

We then clicked on the following hit, which retrieved some pages on XML:

World Wide Web Consortium
Industry consortium with information about the Web for developers and users. Reference software is free to download.

This shows that it is not always easy to map your requirements onto an appropriate category, and sometimes you may not find the information you are looking for if it has been placed in a different category.

When we looked for items on digital libraries, we took the following path:

Library >> Reference >> Libraries & Archives

Under the Libraries & Archives heading, we found the following entries:

- Guides & Directories
- Archives
- Libraries By Subject
- Library Catalogs
- National Libraries
- Library/Info Jobs
- Library Science
- Public Libraries
- University Libraries
- Virtual Libraries.

Although there was no Digital Libraries subcategory, we did find some items on digital libraries, e.g., the Alexandra Digital Library, under Virtual Libraries.

Search in LookSmart

LookSmart searching is very straightforward: users simply enter search terms. According to the Help page, Boolean operators are not necessary. A search produces a list of sites reviewed by LookSmart's editors, with 'see also' suggestions.

Argus Clearinghouse

The Argus Clearinghouse is a relatively small and selective guide to web resources: 'Guides selected for inclusion in the Argus Clearinghouse are representative of the 5-10% of guides submitted which match our selection criteria' (Argus Clearinghouse website). Figure 4.5 shows the Argus Clearinghouse home page.

The following are the main categories of Argus Clearinghouse:

- Arts & Humanities: architecture (cross-listed under Engineering); area studies; cinema; dance; history; languages; literature; museums and galleries; music; occult; performance art; philosophy and religion; visual arts
- Business & Employment: banking and investment; business; economics; employment; finance and credit; human resources; industry; marketing

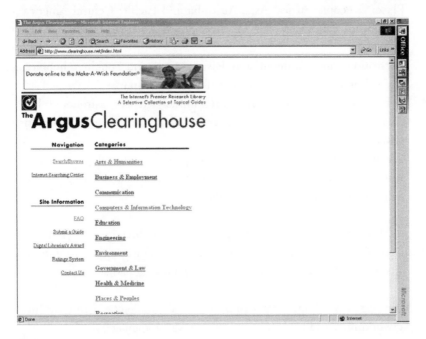

Fig 4.5   *Argus Clearinghouse home page*

- Communication: communications and media studies; journalism and writing; libraries and information science; news media; publishing; telecommunication; television and radio
- Computers & Information Technology: computer science and technologies; computers and computer industry; Internet and networking; software and operating systems
- Education: adult and special education; educational institutions; higher education; instructional technology and tools; primary and secondary school; teaching and pedagogy
- Engineering: architecture (cross-listed under Arts & Humanities); construction; industrial engineering; telecommunications; transportation
- Environment: ecology; environmental activism; environmental law; sustainable development; waste management
- Government & Law: government; intellectual property; law and regulation; military; politics and elections
- Health & Medicine: disabilities; diseases and disorders; fitness and nutrition; general health; medical specialties; medicine and medical services; sexuality and reproduction
- Places & People: Africa; Asia; Australia and Pacific; Central America and Caribbean; Europe; North America; South America; travel and regional information
- Recreation: entertainment and leisure; food and cooking; hobbies and crafts; home and garden; nature activities; pets; sports
- Science & Mathematics: agriculture; animal sciences; astronomy; biology; botany; chemistry; earth sciences; general science; mathematics and statistics; physics
- Social Science & Social Issues: anthropology; archaeology; communities and urban planning; families; linguistics; political science; psychology; social activism; social issues; sociology

Argus Clearinghouse is smaller compared with the three major web directories discussed above, so fewer web pages are covered. For example, we found only five hits when we looked for HTML by the following path:

Main page > > Computers & Information Technology> > Internet and Networking> > HTML (HyperText Markup Language)

When we searched for metadata, we found nothing, while a search on digital libraries retrieved only one guide. However, the hits retrieved are rated, and the directory layout is easy to understand.

Argus Clearinghouse search

When a search command is executed, Argus Clearinghouse searches the full text of the information pages for each of the Argus Clearinghouse guides, including titles, the names of authors, their institutions, and descriptive keywords. A search can be conducted by entering a simple search term or by entering a phrase within double quotes. Boolean AND and OR operators can be used to combine search terms; the NOT operator is not supported. A search term can be truncated by using '*' at the end of a word.

The WWW Virtual Library

The WWW Virtual Library was founded in 1991 by Tim Berners-Lee, the inventor of the web. Its most interesting feature is that each WWW Virtual Library site is maintained by a different institution, and the content is solely the responsibility of the maintainer of that site. The main categories of the WWW Virtual Library are as follows (see Figure 4.6):

- Agriculture
- Business and Economics
- Computing
- Communications and Media
- Education
- Engineering
- Humanities
- Information and Libraries
- International Affairs
- Law
- Recreation
- Regional Studies
- Science
- Society.

From the main page, when we clicked on the Information and Libraries category we obtained the following hierarchy:

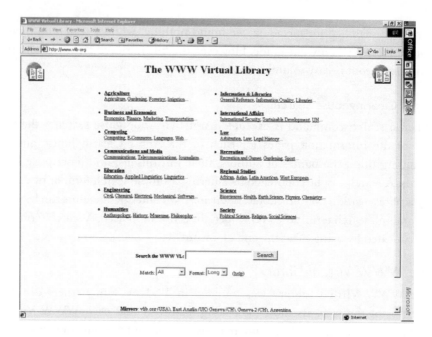

Fig. 4.6 *The WWW Virtual Library home page*

- General Reference
- Information Quality
  - Electronic References and Scholarly Citations of Internet Sources
  - Evaluation of Information Resources
- Knowledge Management
- Library Resources

This hierarchical arrangement of subcategories is different from the other web directories discussed above, and it helps users get a visual representation of the relationships among the various topics. Each of the subcategories is linked to a site offering further information. Similarly, the Computing category has the following hierarchy:

- Artificial Intelligence
- Audio
- Cryptography, PGP and Privacy
- Electronic Commerce
- Formal Methods
- Handheld Computing

- Logic Programming
- Networking Information
- Mobile and Wireless Computing
- Programming Languages
  - Java
  - Tcl and Tk
  - Visual Languages and Programming
- Safety-Critical Systems
- SCSI (Small Computer System Interface)
- Software Engineering
- The Virtual Museum of Computing
- World-Wide Web Development.

The WWW Virtual Library search

The search options on the home page are limited, but the interface is very simple. More advanced search options are given by clicking on 'help' underneath the search box, as follows:

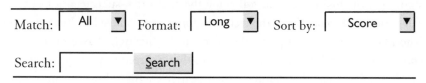

Users can select from the options:

- All – all of the words in the search field (Boolean AND search)
- Any – any of the words in the search field (Boolean OR search)
- Boolean – explicit Boolean search using the AND/OR/NOT operators and parentheses to define the query.

Users can select the format option to decide on the display of search results. There are two options:

- Long – displays the titles, relevant excerpt text, date of last modification and size of the matching pages
- Short – displays just the page titles.

Users can select from the following sort options:

- Score – search result pages are sorted by relevance (most relevant to least)
- Time – search results are sorted by date of last modification (most recent to oldest)
- Title – search results are sorted by title alphabetically (A to Z)
- Reverse Score – search results are sorted by reverse order of relevance (least relevant to most)
- Reverse Time – search results are sorted by reverse order of date of last modification (oldest to most recent)
- Reverse Title – search results are sorted by reverse order of title (Z to A).

Summary

From the discussions of the five web directories, we can derive a number of important points. The basic idea behind web directories is the organization of websites based on a hierarchical representation of their subject contents. Users looking for information on a given topic are required to browse the categories, starting at the main page and following the categories, subcategories, sub-sub-categories, and so on. Since the web directories are managed by human experts who place a website at a particular place in the hierarchy based on its subject content, the overall number of web pages that a directory provides access to is much smaller than that handled by a search engine. However, information resources found through browsing a directory may be more relevant since they have been evaluated and categorized by human experts.

Web directories are very useful tools for users who are not subject experts or experienced web searchers. They are also a good starting point when someone wants to get general information on a given topic. However, web directories also provide search facilities, and expert searchers can take advantage of this. Unlike the search facilities available within a search engine, a searcher can limit a search within a specific category. Some web directories also allow users to search the entire web, or use other search engines 'behind the scene', to get more results.

The major problem of finding information using a web directory is that it can be difficult to choose an appropriate category. If the wrong category is chosen from the main page, then there is less likelihood of finding an appropriate site. We gave several simple examples in this chapter, where we had chosen a specific path in the web directory but could not find appropriate subcategories.

Also sites on the same topic may be placed under two or more different categories, e.g., items on digital libraries have been placed under the Library (or Library & Information Science category) as well as under Computer Science, or even under the main Reference category.

There are significant differences in the way the main categories within directories have been created. These categories, and their subcategories, are not standard across all directories, and consequently a given website may appear at a different part of the hierarchy in two different web directories. Several researchers have shown these differences, and many have also discussed the subjectivity of categorization and the need for a library classification scheme for organizing internet resources. See, for example, Vizine-Goetz (1997); Bates (1998); McKierman (1999) and Lincicum (n.d.).

Another problem with web directories is related to the principles followed in organizing web resources. It is evident that if we need to categorize all web information resources on all subjects or disciplines all over the world, then we shall have serious difficulties. The volume of work would be huge, we would need many human experts in all disciplines, and the overall process would be very resource-intensive. From the user's point-of-view such a huge directory of resources would be difficult to browse through. In order to deal with this problem, web directories have been developed that concentrate on a specific subject area, and are particularly suitable for users in a specific discipline. These subject gateways are discussed in Chapter 5.

Chapter 5
Subject gateways

Introduction

Subject gateways are essentially online libraries containing links and pages on a variety of categorized topics. Similar, in a very general way, to web directories, they are a good resource for users trying to do serious online research on a specific area of interest (Bradley, 1999). Subject gateways are also known as virtual libraries, gateways, digital collections, cyber libraries, and so on (Bradley, 1999; Oregon State University Virtual Libraries website). In this book we use the term subject gateway, since many cover a specific subject or discipline. Each subject gateway contains a great deal of information on its given subject. It may contain a variety of information such as: full-text documents, resource guides, bibliographies, directories, mailing lists and newsgroups, links to other websites, news about new items or events, and so on. A number of publications discuss virtual libraries, and provide checklists for subject gateways confined to a particular country or subject. See, for example, Bradley (1999); Campbell (2000); Dempsey (2000); Fischer and Neuroth (2000); Granum and Barker (2000); Heery (2000); Hiom (2000); Koch (2000); MacLeod (2000); Missingham, (2000) and Price (2000).

Subject gateway principles

Bradley (1999) suggests that virtual libraries or subject gateways information contained are characterized by the facts that (1) the information contained in them is more important than their geographical location, (2) they are kept current, and (3) information professionals and subject experts put their knowledge and expertise to collate information on specific subjects.

The subject gateway approach to organizing access to internet resources has been in existence – in various guises and under various names – since the mid-1990s (OMNI website). The fundamentals of this approach are that:

- various internet resources are selected by human experts for their quality and relevance to a particular target audience
- these are then reviewed and resource descriptions created, which are stored, generally with the associated metadata, and generally in a structured format.

Efforts are made to improve the recall and especially the precision of information searching on the web by users in a particular subject or discipline. In the UK the most high profile and successful gateway developments have been those supported by the JISC (Joint Information Systems Committee) eLib programme, including EEVL (for engineering), OMNI (health and biomedicine) and SOSIG (social sciences) (OMNI website). A large number of gateways have been developed in recent years, and a useful subject list – though not comprehensive – is provided at the end of this chapter.

Subject gateways in specific disciplines

In this section we shall describe the features of some subject gateways that deal with specific disciplines.

Social sciences

SOSIG, the Social Science Information Gateway, aims to provide researchers and practitioners in the field of social sciences, business and law with access to high-quality internet information. It uses social science academics and information specialists who select and describe sites after evaluation of their quality. Figure 5.1 shows the SOSIG home page, Figure 5.2 shows the social science search engine and Figure 5.3 shows the SOSIG catalogue.

The following are some important features of SOSIG:

- Subject coverage: social sciences
- Language: English
- Content selectors: academic
- Classification: the Universal Decimal Classification (UDC)
- Thesaurus: HASSET thesaurus, developed by The Data Archive

Fig. 5.1   *SOSIG home page*

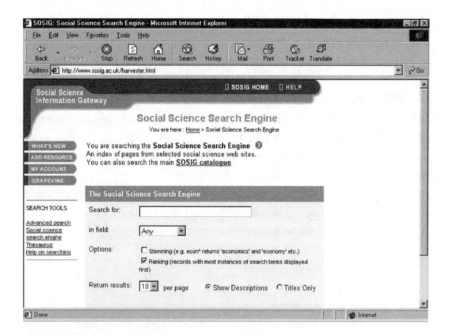

Fig. 5.2   *SOSIG social science search engine*

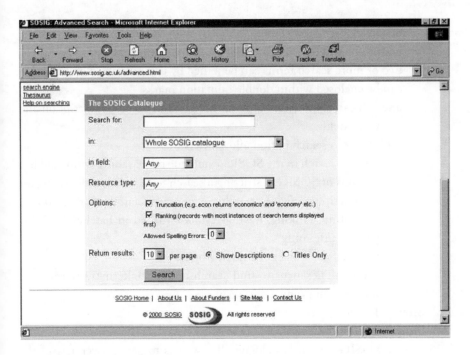

Fig. 5.3 *SOSIG catalogue*

- Type of resource: articles/papers/reports (collections), articles/papers/reports (individual), bibliographic databases, bibliographies, books/book equivalents, companies, company information, datasets, documents (digests, law reports, legislation, treatises), educational materials, FAQs, government publications, government bodies, journals (contents and abstracts), mailing lists/discussion groups, news, organizations/societies, software, research projects/centres, reference materials, resource guides, and journals (full text)
- Searchable: yes
- Search features
  - the catalogue is searchable by subject area
  - either the SOSIG catalogue (which contains internet resources selected by the SOSIG team) or the Social Science Search Engine (an index of pages from over 50,000 social science websites) can be searched
  - simple keyword search is possible
  - users can restrict their search to a subject section of SOSIG by using an option
  - users can search for specific URLs by default from the general search box,

or can choose to search only for URLs from the advanced search box
- both right and left truncation of the search term is possible
- two or more search terms can be joined by using Boolean operators, or can be enclosed within double quotation marks
- a search can be restricted to terms held within the title, description and keywords fields
- the advanced search option allows users to:
  (a) refine a search in the SOSIG catalogue by searching within subject sections of SOSIG, restricting a search to either the title, keywords or description fields, searching for particular types of resource, truncating, ranking, having results returned in batches, and displaying titles only
  (b) use the Social Science Search Engine
  (c) use the Thesaurus to find search terms or alternative terms, if a search term produces no results
- Browsable: yes
- Browse features
  - the SOSIG internet catalogue allows users to get an overview of the resources available
  - browsing is possible within a region (such as World, Europe or UK)
  - lists of resources can be viewed either alphabetically or by resource type
  - the catalogue is browsable by subject area
- Display results
  - results are displayed in batches. The default is 10 but users have options to change this to 5, 20 or 50, or to get all the results listed on a single page
  - results can be displayed by titles only, but the title, description, keywords and URL of resources are displayed by default
- Special features
  - browsing/searching can be restricted to a particular geographical region
  - users can create their own personal view of the web ('My Account'): they can find out which resources have recently been added in their area, and can register for regular e-mail notification of important developments
  - the SOSIG subject and alphabetical index can be used to look for information easily
  - other SOSIG services include: document archive (annual reports, paper and articles, subject guides are available), internet detective, planet SOSIG, and SOSIG mailing list.

Business and economics

Biz/ed, the Business and Economics information gateway, is described as a unique service for students, teachers and lecturers in business and economics. The site allows users either to browse resource descriptions within subject headings or to use keyword searching of the descriptions. Figure 5.4 shows the search screen of Biz/ed.

Biz/ed contains five sections as follows:

1 The Internet Catalogue contains over 2300 selected resources described by subject experts. The Biz/ed database is regularly updated and new resources added.

2 The Learning Materials section contains a large number of worksheets and other primary materials that help users to find relevant materials in business studies and economics. Users need to select the subject they are interested in and then the topic that relates to their area of study or teaching.

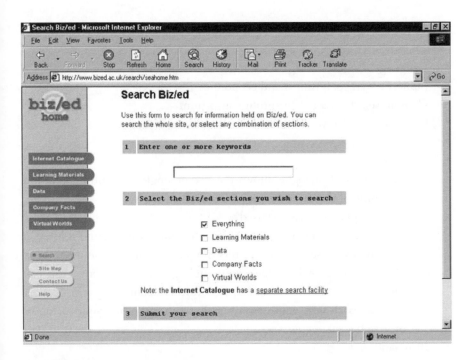

Fig. 5.4 *Biz/ed search screen*

3   Data: Biz/ed hosts both original and mirrored datasets for economics, business and finance for the UK and overseas. Resources are divided by the source of data, and each section contains its own instructions on how to use and get the most out of the data available.

4   In the Company Facts section, 12 leading companies and organizations provide answers to the questions that are most frequently asked by students. The easiest way to use this section is to simply click on a specific company. This will take the user to a list of frequently asked questions collected within key business studies disciplines. There is also a search facility.

5   Virtual Worlds is divided into two sections: the Virtual Factory and the Virtual Economy. The Virtual Factory is a web page that contains links to all those types of information that one may need in the context of a business, and has been designed according to the various stages of a business, such as business planning, production, accounts, marketing, and so on. The Virtual Economy is an interesting web page containing information related to economics and finance. It is organized according to the various floors and sections of the UK Chancellor's Office.

The following are essential features of Biz/ed:

- Language: English
- Subject coverage: business and economics
- Content selectors: a not-for-profit consortium
- Classification: Dewey Decimal Classification (DDC)
- Searchable: yes
- Search features:
    - the Internet Catalogue allows the use of single or multiple keyword searching of the descriptions
    - Boolean operators can be used
    - a list of resource records with the number of resources found is listed at the top, if your search term results in up to 100 matches. A description of the resource will include your highlighted search term. You can select the title of the resource to view further details.
    - if your search term returns no matches you can refine your search or browse the catalogue.
- Browsable: yes
- Browse features:

- the Internet Catalogue allows users to browse resource descriptions within subject headings
- you can get a quick overview of what is available on a certain subject by browsing the Internet Catalogue
- use the list of subject headings to find resources in your area of interest
- the results will be presented as a list of titles
- select the name of a resource from the listing to jump to a short description of the website or select the icon to connect to the service directly.
- Display results: in the Internet Catalogue, search results can be displayed only with titles or with descriptions (which include keywords and source), whereas in other sections, such as Learning Materials, search results are displayed with titles and a line to describe the content of a document.
- Special features:
  - you can search the whole site, or select any combination of sections
  - the Internet Catalogue has its own search facility
  - a list of possible keywords has been prepared as a quick reference tool to assist searching
  - if your search term results in more than 100 matches you will be asked to return to the search page and submit a request with more specific search terms.

Engineering

EEVL, Edinburgh Engineering Virtual Library, provides a central access point to networked engineering information for the UK higher education and research community. It is a free service, created and run by a team of information specialists from Heriot-Watt University, with input from many other UK universities. The site features a catalogue of selected engineering resources, targeted engineering search engines, bibliographic and events databases, an engineering on the internet bibliography, links to useful sites, and so on. The EEVL Catalogue has over 5000 reviews of the best engineering internet sites. EEVL covers a wide range of engineering subjects, which includes: aerospace and defence engineering, bioengineering, chemical engineering, civil engineering, electrical, electronic and computer engineering, engineering design, environmental engineering, materials engineering, mechanical and manufacturing engineering, nanotechnology and petroleum and offshore engineering. Figures 5.5 and 5.6 show the EEVL home page, and Figures 5.7 and 5.8 show its browse and search screens respectively.

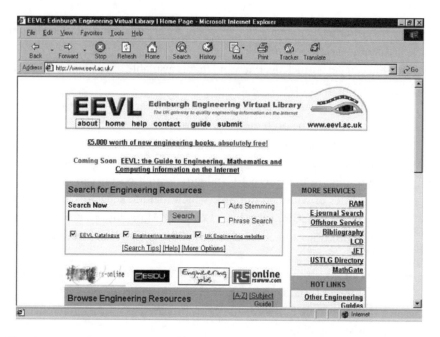

Fig. 5.5 *EEVL home page (top)*

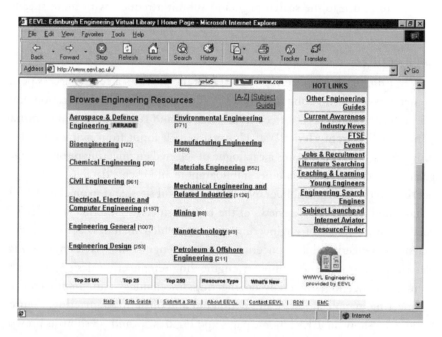

Fig. 5.6 *EEVL home page (bottom)*

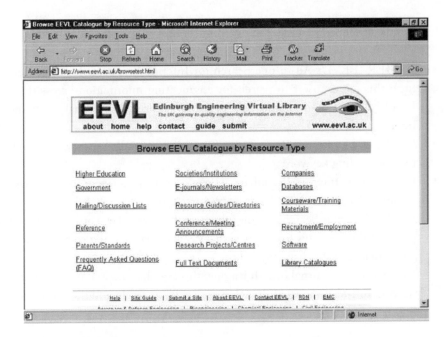

Fig. 5.7   *EEVL browse by resource type*

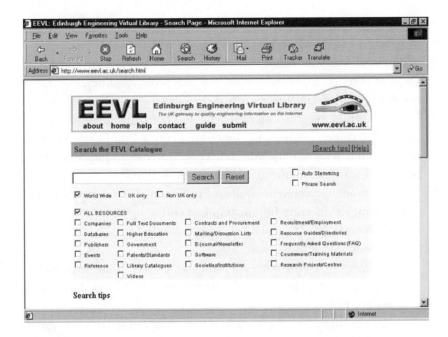

Fig. 5.8   *EEVL search screen*

EEVL has developed a number of different services:

- EASIER (EEVL's All-in-one Search for Internet Resources for Engineering): this allows users to search for engineering information across three EEVL databases simultaneously to locate information available on the internet
- Catalogue of Internet Resources – Searching: this allows users to search resources using keywords
- Catalogue of Internet Resources – Browsing: this allows users to browse resources by subject heading or by resource type
- UK Engineering Search Engine: this searches every keyword on the web pages of the UK sites listed in the EEVL Catalogue, and also all the web pages that are referenced from those pages
- Engineering E-Journal Search Engine: this searches the web pages of engineering full-text e-journal sites that are available freely and do not require registration.

The following are the essential features of EEVL:

- Language: English
- Subject coverage: engineering
- Content selectors: academic
- Type of resource: higher education, research projects/centres, full-text documents, library catalogues, e-journals/newsletters, resource guides/directories, companies, government, societies/institutions, mailing/discussion lists, databases, conference/meeting announcements, recruitment/employment information, patents/standards, reference materials, courseware/training materials, software, frequently asked questions (FAQ)
- Classification: homegrown, based on Engineering Information Inc. (Ei)
- Thesaurus: Engineering Information Inc. (Ei)
- Searchable: yes
- Search features:
  - you can search for resources in particular sectors (e.g. commercial/higher academic sector) or of a particular type (e.g. an e-journal, courseware, mailing list)
  - you can find resources using keywords. You can refine your search by using Boolean operators (AND, OR, NOT), truncation, phrase search-

ing or multiple word combinations. You can also limit your search to only UK sites, and by resource type (e.g. e-journal, higher education site, training materials etc). This is also searched by EASIER

- you can search the Engineering Newsgroup Archive by content, newsgroup, subject or author
- you can search the EEVL Catalogue, EEVL's Engineering Newsgroup Archive or UK Engineering websites
- you can restrict your search within that resource type by selecting Resource Filter
- EEVL provides a search engine of freely available full-text engineering e-journals – both scholarly and trade

- Browsable: yes
- Browse features:
  - you can browse by resource type. You can restrict your browsing to resources in particular sectors (e.g. commercial/higher academic sector) or of a particular type (e.g. an e-journal, courseware, mailing list)
  - you can browse resources by subject headings: there are 46 of these, grouped into 10 main categories. To browse by subject, click on the Browse button which will take you to a listing in a particular subject area
  - reviews can also be browsed by subject or type e.g. full-text papers, higher education, recruitment, e-journal, research projects, etc.
  - if you can't find what you are looking for in specific categories, then check in the General section
  - you can browse resources by location (UK or non-UK resources)
- Display results: results are displayed in slightly different ways because each database stores different kinds of information – descriptions of websites/internet resources, newsgroup postings and web pages
- Special features:
  - other services include: Recent Advances in Manufacturing bibliographic database, Offshore Engineering Information Service, Bibliography of Engineering Internet Guides
  - context-specific Further Advice pages are available from the bottom of the browse pages, which point to other resource listings in different subject areas, as well as links to the EEVL Engineering Newsgroup Archive and UK Engineering Search Engine
  - further help with searching is available
  - the services searched by EASIER can also be searched individually

–   the USTLG (University Science & Technology Librarians Group) Directory, a database searchable by name, institution and subject area, is available
–   a listing of the content of each subject heading is available.

EELS, Engineering E-Library, Sweden, is an information system for quality assessed information resources on the internet. It is mainly designed to provide access to engineering internet resources. In addition to the subject coverage, the selection criteria include other features of sites such as the accessibility, maintenance, documentation and reliability. Most of the selected EELS resources are free, but some are restricted to password access and are not available free. Figures 5.9 and 5.10 show the EELS home page, and Figures 5.11 and 5.12 show two EELS search screens.

The following are the essential features of EELS:

•   Language: by default a search will retrieve documents in any language, but the user may choose to limit results to either English or Swedish documents
•   Subject coverage: engineering

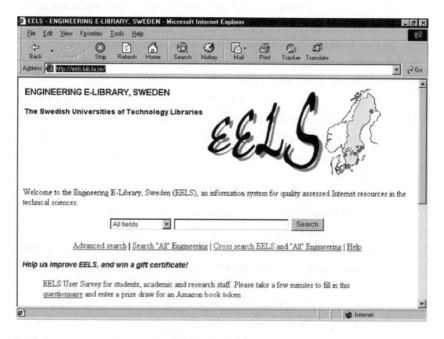

Fig. 5.9   *EELS home page (top)*

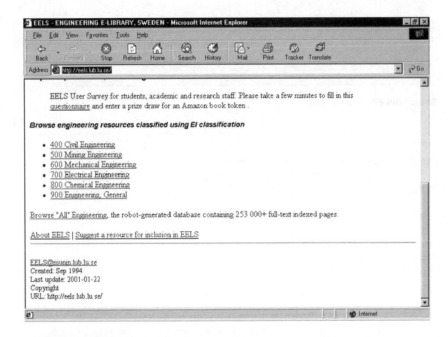

Fig. 5.10 *EELS home page (bottom)*

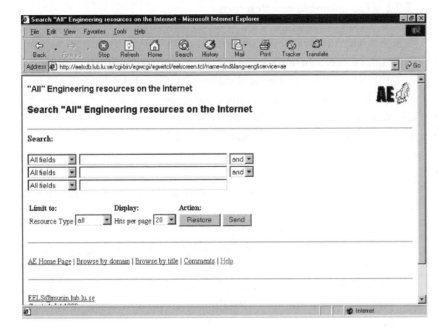

Fig. 5.11 *EELS internet search screen*

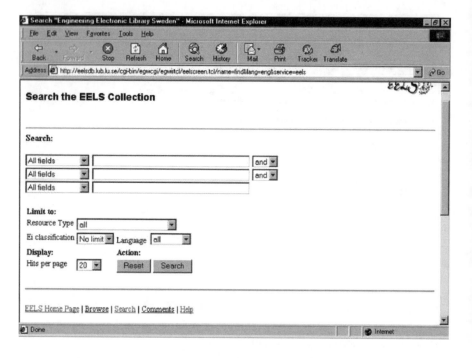

Fig. 5.12 *EELS advanced search screen*

- Content selectors: academic
- Type of resource: dictionaries, e-journals, electronic conferences, directories, full-text databases, image databases, statistical databases, publication lists, tables of contents, bibliographic databases, and so on
- Classification: Engineering Information Inc. (Ei)
- Thesaurus: Engineering Information Inc. (Ei)
- Searchable: yes
- Search features:
    - you may narrow your search to a particular branch of the Ei classification system
    - you can search by resource type
    - you can narrow a search by title, subject, URL, language, Ei classification, and resource type
    - truncation in any part of a word is supported
    - you can search the title, description, Ei classification, subject, URL fields
    - you can enter a word or phrase in each of the input fields. You may

include truncation in the search terms. The additional fields that may be searched are title, description and URL. It may help to bear in mind you are searching both a robot created index ('All' engineering) and a catalogue with evaluation and classification provided by subject specialists

- Browsable: yes
- Browse features: you can navigate through the Ei hierarchical classification system by using the links to the next higher or the next lower level of the hierarchy, starting from a chosen subject page
- Display results: search results can be displayed by 5, 10, 15, 20, 25, 50, and 100 per page
- Special features: EELS has an automatically generated, searchable index, limited to subject-specific resources.

Medicine

OMNI, Organizing Medical Networked Information, is described as a gateway to evaluated, quality internet resources in health and medicine, aimed at students, researchers, academics and practitioners in the health and medical sciences. It has been created by a team of information specialists and subject experts based at the University of Nottingham Greenfield Medical Library, in collaboration with key organizations throughout the UK and further afield, and is one of the gateways within the BIOME service (BIOME web page). Figure 5.13 shows the OMNI advanced search screen.

The following are the essential features of OMNI:

- Language: English
- Subject coverage: medicine, biomedicine, allied health, health management and related topics
- Content selectors: academic
- Type of resource: journals (full text, contents and abstracts), resource guide, bibliographic databases, books, software, organizations, documents/reports, mailing lists, patient information leaflets, non-bibliographic databases, botanical garden, learning materials, news service, position statements, practice guidelines, and systematic reviews
- Classification: National Library of Medicine (NLM)
- Thesaurus: Medical Subject Headings (MeSH)
- Searchable: yes

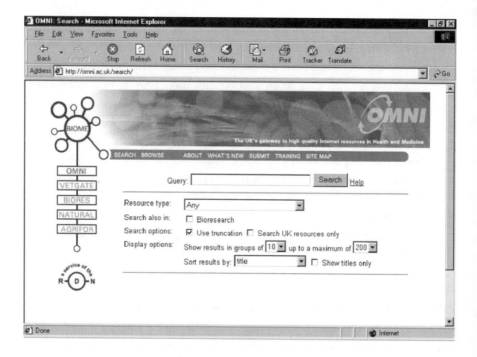

Fig. 5.13 *OMNI advanced search screen*

- Search features:
  - you can search the descriptions of internet resources
  - simple searching is possible either by word search, Boolean search, or by phrase search
  - truncation is possible
  - you can search several other catalogues of types of internet-based biomedical resources, either individually, or in some combination with the main OMNI catalogue
- Browsable: yes
- Browse features:
  - you can browse by classification scheme using NLM, which gives you a broad overview of the range of subject areas
  - you can browse by using MeSH keywords
- Display results: users can display the results by title or by title within gateway
- Special features:
  - OMNI staff can provide training workshops, demonstrations, speakers and consultancy, on a range of subjects concerning biomedical infor-

mation on the internet, tailored to your needs
- the OMNI mailing list provides a forum for disseminating news and discussion about the service
- there is a section on SAGE (Special Advisory Group on Evaluation), a group of people that have advised OMNI, BIOME and the wider community on matters concerning the evaluation of internet-based resources. The group has produced a list of evaluation criteria, as well as several articles and papers, which are reproduced or linked here.

General subject gateways

There are some subject gateways that provide a value-added information service for more than one subject. Examples of these are discussed below.

NOVAGate, Nordic Gateway to Information in Forestry, Veterinary and Agricultural Sciences, is a gateway to selected internet resources in the fields of forestry, veterinary, agricultural, food and environmental sciences. In the database you will find descriptions of and links to databases (bibliographic and full-text), directories, events, internet resource guides, training material, and websites of key organizations, within the above subject areas. The database covers Nordic resources as well as European resources and those of international organizations. Figure 5.14 shows the home page of NOVAGate, and Figures 5.15 and 5.16 show the browse and search screens.

The following are the essential features of NOVAGate:

- Language: Nordic languages and English
- Subject coverage: forestry, veterinary and agricultural sciences
- Content selectors: the libraries of the NOVA University, a co-operative project between the veterinary and agricultural universities in Denmark, Finland, Iceland, Norway and Sweden
- Type of resource: databases, directories, events, resource guides, organizations, and training materials
- Thesaurus: Agrovoc (FAO)
- Searchable: yes
- Search features:
  - searches are made in the titles, alternative title, descriptions and subject words of each resource in the database

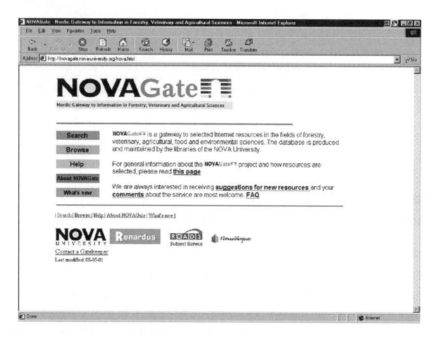

Fig. 5.14 *NOVAgate home page*

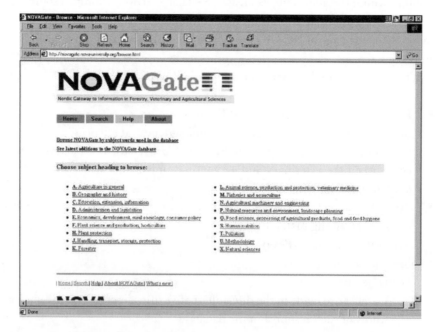

Fig. 5.15 *NOVAgate browse page*

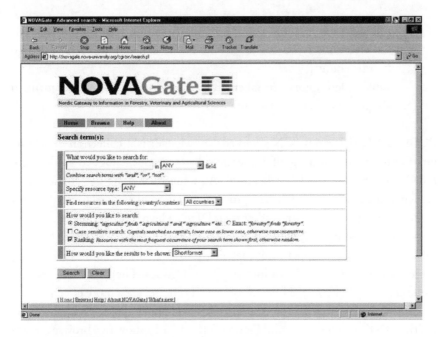

Fig. 5.16 *NOVAgate search page*

- – in the simple search, type your search term(s) in the first box and press the Search button below
- – searches can be combined, and are matched with terms found in individual resource descriptions in the database
- – in the more specific search, searches can be refined by narrowing down a search to a specific field, or to a specific type of resource or to a specific country
- – you can conduct an exact search, using stemming, case sensitivity or ranking
- • Browsable: yes, there is a broad subject structure
- • Browse features:
  - – browse by the subject words given to each resource
  - – browse by broad subject category
- • Display results: search results can be displayed either in a short format (only titles, English description and internet addresses, URLs) or in a detailed format (all fields)
- • Special features:
  - – the database covers Nordic resources as well as European resources and those of international organizations

– cataloguers search the internet regularly to find relevant and substantial electronic resources to include in the database in each of the five Nordic countries

– subject descriptors are taken from the Agrovoc (FAO) thesaurus, in English, Finnish or Danish.

BUBL LINK (Libraries of Networked Knowledge) is a collection of selected internet resources covering all academic subject areas, catalogued according to DDC (Dewey Decimal Classification). All items are selected, evaluated, catalogued and described. BUBL 5:15 provides an alternative interface to this catalogue, based on subject terms rather than DDC. The name 5:15 refers to its aim to guarantee a minimum of 5 and maximum of 15 relevant resources for every subject; however, the upper limit may go up to 35 items for some subjects. Big subject areas are broken down into smaller categories. The BUBL LINK catalogue currently holds over 11,000 resources. It can provide a more effective route to information for many subjects, across all disciplines. Figure 5.17 shows the BUBL LINK search screen, and Figures 5.18 and 5.19 show two browse screens.

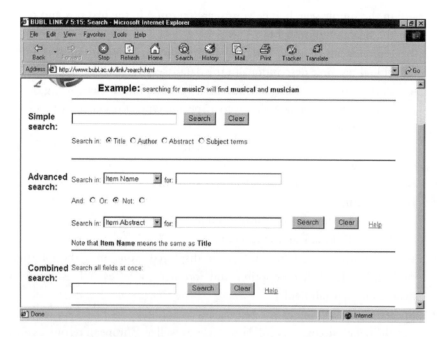

Fig. 5.17 *BUBL LINK search screen*

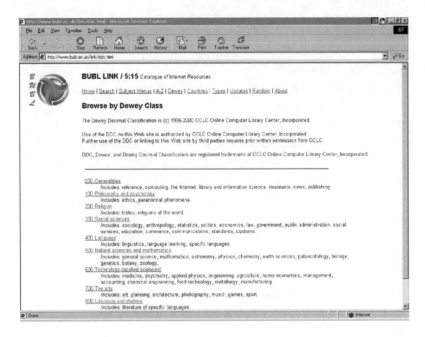

Fig. 5.18 *BUBL LINK DDC browse screen*

Fig. 5.19 *BUBL LINK subject browse screen*

The following are the essential features of BUBL LINK:

- Language: English
- Subject coverage: all
- Content selectors: academic
- Type of resource (general reference): directories, dictionaries, bibliographies, thesauri, reference data/documents, JISC funded services and projects, mailing lists, bookshops, biographies, library catalogues, UK university home pages, UK higher education colleges, other UK institutions, governments worldwide, book and text collections, essays, poems, proceedings, magazine listings, journal listings, journal collections, guides/tutorials/teaching materials, image collections, map collections, moving images, museums, satellite images, software archives, sound collections
- Classification: Dewey Decimal Classification (DDC)
- Thesaurus: originally based on LCSH (Library of Congress Subject Headings)
- Searchable: yes
- Search features:
    - general keyword search (searches all fields), single field search (searches only within one field), and advanced search (searches a combination of fields)
    - the single field search has five searchable fields: item name, author, item abstract, subjects (free-text subject headings assigned to a resource or service, based on LCSH where suitable), and DDC number
    - the general keyword search scans the LINK database for all occurrences of the search term irrespective of the field
    - the advanced search allows you to build Boolean searches and to specify the catalogue fields of the LINK database to be searched. A list of catalogue fields available for searching is displayed by selecting index field: item name, item content type, item abstract, author, author type, subjects, resource type, location, and date
    - both left and right truncation can be carried out in searching; adjacency searches are not supported
- Browsable: either by subject or by Dewey class
- Browse features:
    - you can browse by Dewey class
    - you can browse by subject

- Display results: search results are displayed by title and description, along with author, subjects, Dewey class, resource type, and location
- Special features: the advanced search form is used to search the Acqlink service for acquisitions librarians.

Summary

Table 5.1 presents a quick overview of some selected features of seven subject gateways. Subject gateways have been created to help users browse and search selected information resources on the web. They aim to overcome some of the problems of web search engines by focusing on a specific discipline and by following more stringent selection and evaluation criteria. One of the major characteristics of the gateways discussed in this chapter, as opposed to the web directories discussed in Chapter 4, is that they often use the expertise of library and information professionals who have long been engaged in handling and organizing reference and information resources. The results of a search using a subject gateway may be much smaller compared with those obtained using a large web search engine or directory, but they are often more accurate and up to date, since they are selected and evaluated by human experts.

A select list of subject gateways

ADAM: Art, Design, Architecture & Media Information Gateway
(http://adam.ac.uk/)
   A 'searchable catalogue of . . . internet resources that have been carefully selected and catalogued by professional librarians for the benefit of the UK Higher Education community'.

AGRIGATE: Agriculture Information Gateway for Australian Researchers
(http://www.agrigate.edu.au/)
   A collection of agricultural resources which can be browsed by selecting broad headings, searched by entering a keyword or phrase, or accessed via a controlled list of subject terms, assigned to describe agribusiness, farming systems, aquaculture, field crops, food sciences, meteorology and viticulture.

BeCal: Belief, Culture and Learning Information Gateway
(http://www.becal.net/)
   Contains peer-reviewed educational and research resources concerning belief, culture and values.

Table 5.1 *Features of seven selected subject gateways*

Name	Language	Subject coverage	Content selectors	Classification	Thesaurus	Type of Resource
SOSIG	English	Social sciences	Academic	Universal Decimal Classification (UDC)	HASSET thesaurus, developed by The Data Archive	Articles/papers/reports (collections), articles/papers/reports (individual), bibliographic databases, bibliographies, books, company information, datasets, digests, law reports, legislation, treatises, educational materials, FAQs (frequently asked questions), government publications, government bodies, journals (contents, abstracts and full texts), mailing lists/discussion groups, news, organizations/societies, software, research projects, reference materials, resource guides
Biz/ed	English	Business and economics	Not-for-profit consortium	Dewey Decimal Classification System (DDC)	Homegrown thematic grouping of keywords	Internet resources in the areas of business, management and economics; learning materials (suitable for students at different levels) in the subjects of business, economics and accounting; company data and facts
EEVL	English	Engineering	Academic	Homegrown; based on the Engineering Information Inc's Ei classification	Engineering Information Inc thesaurus	Higher education research projects/centres, full text documents, library catalogue, e-journals/newsletters, resource guides/ directories, companies, government, societies/ institutions, mailing/discussion lists, databases, conference/meeting announcements, recruitment/

(continued)

Table 5.1 (continued)

Name	Language	Subject coverage	Content selectors	Classification	Thesaurus	Type of Resource
						employment, patents, standards, reference books, courseware/training materials, software, FAQs
OMNI	English	Medicine, bio-medicine, allied health, health management and related topics	Academic	National Library of Medicine (NLM) Classification	Medical Subject Headings (MeSH) thesaurus	Journals - contents, abstracts and full text, resource guide, bibliographic database, book, software, organization, documents/report, mailing list, patient information leaflet , non-bibliographic database, botanical garden, learning materials, news service, position statement, practice guidelines, and systematic review
EELS	If a user doesn't specify otherwise, a search will retrieve documents in any language. However, the user may choose instead to limit the results to either English or Swedish documents	Engineering	Academic	Engineering Information Inc's Ei classification	Engineering Information Inc's Ei thesaurus	Dictionaries, electronic journals, electronic conferences, directories, , full-text database, image database, statistical database, publication list, table of contents, bibliographic database

(continued)

Table 5.1 (continued)

Name	Language	Subject coverage	Content selectors	Classification	Thesaurus	Type of Resource
NOVAGate	Nordic languages and English	Forestry, veterinary and agricultural sciences	The libraries of the NOVA University - a cooperative project between the veterinary and agricultural universities in Denmark, Finland, Iceland, Norway and Sweden	Nil	Agrovoc (FAO: Food and Agricultural Organization) thesaurus	Database, directory, event, resource guide, organization, and training materials
BUBL Link	English	All	Academic	Dewey Decimal Classification (DDC)	Originally based on LCSH (Library of Congress Subject Headings) but has been customized and expanded to suit the content of the BUBL service	General reference: directories, dictionaries, bibliographies, thesauri, reference data/documents, JISC funded services and projects, mailing lists, bookshops, biographies, library catalogues, UK university home pages, UK higher education colleges, other UK institutions, governments worldwide, book and text collections, essays, poems, proceedings, magazine listings, journal listings, journal collections, guides/ tutorials/teaching materials, image collections, map collections, moving images, museums, satellite images, software archives, sound collections.

Chemistry Societies Network Gateway (http://www.chemsoc.org/)
Provides links to chemistry societies, teaching resources, conference information, chemistry services, and news and chemistry related businesses. A search facility is provided, as are more general chemistry links and a current awareness service.

ECOM: Electronic Commerce Research Gateway
(http://ecom.infm.ulst.ac.uk/)
A gateway to electronic commerce research resources on the internet, aimed at informatics and business students as well as companies interested in electronic commerce, internet intelligence and internet marketing.

ELVIL: European Legislative Virtual Library (http://www.sub.se/elvil.htm)
A project aiming to significantly increase the availability of information on European law and politics; it is part of the European Union's Library Programme.

GEM: The Gateway to Educational Materials (http://www.thegateway.org/)
A gateway to educational resources, containing internet-based lesson plans, curriculum units and other educational materials. Contents may be retrieved by title, subject, keyword, education level or catalogue record.

HUMBUL Gateway (http://www.humbul.ac.uk)
A large collection of high-quality links to scholarly resources in the humanities.

Hypertext Webster Gateway
(http://work.ucsd.edu:5141/cgi-bin/http_webster)
A simple interface for accessing various dictionary services on the internet. Search words are entered, producing a list of definitions of the word.

Infolaw: Information for Lawyers Limited's Gateway to the UK Legal
Internet (http://www.infolaw.co.uk/)
A gateway to a variety of legal resources in the UK, including law firms, associations, government information and law schools. It also contains Lawfinder, a resource for researching and keeping up to date with primary law on the web, and which has links to statutes, statutory instruments, bills, consultative documents, parliamentary proceedings, and judgements from the House of Lords, the Court of Appeal and the High Court. A subject-based directory provides further access to electronic legal resources.

Landscape Architecture Virtual Library (http://cala.umn.edu/)
An index of information about landscape architecture, including an inter-

national list of colleges and universities, research, mailing lists, news, software and jobs.

Library of Congress WWW/Z39.50 Gateway
(http://lcweb.loc.gov/z3950/gateway.html)
Links to various ANSI Z39.50 Standard resources that relate to searching databases that have implemented Z39.50; access to many Z39.50 servers is provided through this gateway.

PICK (http://www.aber.ac.uk/~tplwww/e/)
A gateway to quality librarianship and information science resources.

PINAKES: A Subject Launchpad
(http://www.hw.ac.uk/libWWW/irn/pinakes/pinakes.html)
Provides links to most of the major internet subject gateways.

PORT (http://www.port.nmm.ac.uk)
The UK National Maritime Museum's online catalogue of high-quality maritime-related internet resources. Every resource has been selected and described by a librarian or subject specialist. Services and materials developed by the Museum's Centre for Maritime Research are also available on this site.

Poultry Science Virtual Library (http://gallus.tamu.edu/library/dother.html)
An index of information about poultry. Includes lists of universities, research centres, associations, poultry producers and breeding farms.

Royal Society of New Zealand: Gateway to New Zealand Science
(http://www.rsnz.govt.nz/)
News, events, publications and other documentation that reflect the input of the Society into education, policy advice to government, and involvement with NZ science and technology organizations. Includes text of the code of professional standards and ethics.

SciCentral: Gateway to Science and Engineering Online Resources
(http://www.sciquest.com/cgi-bin/ncommerce3/ExecMacro/sci_index.
d2w/report)
A gateway to over 50,000 sites pertaining to over 120 subjects in science and engineering. It is maintained by professional scientists whose mission is to identify and centralize access to the most valuable scientific resources online. Major subject divisions include biological sciences, health sciences, physical and chemical sciences, engineering sciences, women and minorities in science, and science in the news.

Virtual Computer Library (http://www.utexas.edu/computer/vcl/)

Provides pointers to information about computers and computing. Topics covered include academic computing, book reviews, FAQs, publishers and journals.

**Waste Water Engineering Virtual Library
(http://www.cleanh2o.com/cleanh2o/ww/welcome.html)**
The section of the Virtual Library dedicated to wastewater engineering, with options leading to categories of internet-based resources, the ROADS-based searchable catalogue, a HyperNews forum and a section for people to submit relevant resources. The ROADS-based section has a searchable catalogue of around 300 WWE resources.

WWW Virtual Library: Agriculture (http://vlib.org/agriculture.html)
An index of links about agriculture, including agricultural economics, horticultural information, livestock, plant biology and irrigation.

WWW Virtual Library: Computing (http://vlib.org/computing.html)
An index to numerous computing resources, including university departments, institutes, magazines, and particular systems.

WWW Virtual Library: Engineering (http://vlib.org/engineering.html)
A classified list of worldwide engineering resources.

WWW Virtual Library: Humanities (http://vlib.org/humanities.html)
Links to internet resources in the humanities.

WWW Virtual Library: Law (http://vlib.org/law.html)
A collection of subject-related websites around the world, each administering a different subject. Material is arranged by organization type (e.g. US government servers) and by legal topic (e.g. contracts).

WWW Virtual Library: Music (http://www.vl-music.com/)
The music section of the WWW Virtual Library.

Chapter 6
Reference and information services on the web

Introduction

The internet and world wide web have brought significant improvements in the provision of reference and information services. While current awareness and selective dissemination of information (SDI) services have been made available to remote users by various online database services, and organizations such as the Institute of Scientific Information (ISI), long before the appearance of the internet, many new web-based reference and information services are now available. These can now be categorized into three broad groups:

- reference and information services from publishers, database search services and specialized institutions
- reference services provided by libraries and/or experts through the internet
- reference and information services whereby users conduct a web search to find information.

Chowdhury and Chowdhury (2001) discussed several online information services that belong to the first category mentioned above. It includes various current awareness and SDI services, such as:

- contents page services from commercial publishers, such as Elsevier's Contents Direct Service, and IDEAL Alert (see also p. 118)

- information on new books, available free from publishers and vendors, such as the Wiley Book Notification Service and Amazon.com
- SDI services from online search service providers, such as Dialog Alerts
- current contents and alerting services from ISI, and so on.

Some of these services, particularly the contents page services from publishers of journals, are free, while others, such as the Dialog Alerts or Current Contents from ISI, require registration and payment.

Online reference services provided by librarians and experts

Many reference and information services are now provided by librarians and subject experts through the internet. Users ask a question on a web page, or through an e-mail, which is answered via e-mail. While some of these services are provided by libraries to their users, many others are commercial ventures. Many of the commercial services are free, but for some users have to pay. We shall discuss the features of some of these reference services below.

Ask a Librarian

This is a web-based reference service, primarily designed for UK residents, provided by the EARL Consortium for Public Library Networking. A user's query is automatically routed from the enquiry page to one of the participating reference libraries, which receives it as an e-mail message. The library will send the user, within two days, an e-mail message with their response. The home page (see Figure 6.1) provides some basic information for users; Figure 6.2 shows the enquiry page where users enter their questions.

AskTiARA

This is a reference service provided by TiARA (Timely Information for All, Relevant and Affordable), a web-based information service developed in Singapore for local users (see p. 104). Users send reference queries by e-mail. These are directed to the National Library Board's Reference Point. Staff there provide answers through e-mail, usually on the same or the following day.

Fig. 6.1 *Ask a Librarian home page*

Fig. 6.2 *Ask a Librarian enquiry page*

Web-based reference services where experts provide answers

A number of web-based reference and information services have been introduced where a question, asked by a user, is answered by an expert. Some of these services charge users for the service; in some cases experts bid to provide an answer to a question, and the user can select the lowest bid.

AskMe

This is a very interesting free service where a user can simply ask a question and get answers from experts. Users enter their question and their e-mail address, though they can choose not to reveal the latter and thus remain anonymous. Figure 6.3 shows the AskMe home page.

First a user needs to join by entering an e-mail address. AskMe then sends the user an ID and a password, and the user can then start asking questions right away, by entering a subject or browsing a list of categories. For each category that appears on the first page (see Figure 6.3) there is another page listing all the subcategories, and a search box. Users can ask a question using the search box, and can obtain a list of previously asked questions on the topic as well as the answers (see Figure 6.4).

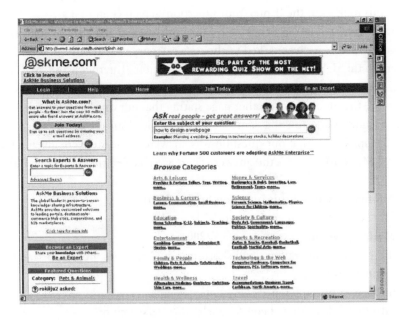

Fig. 6.3   *AskMe.com homepage*

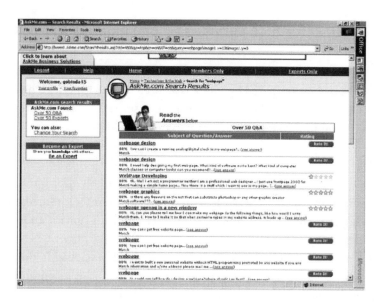

Fig. 6.4 *Answers from AskMe.com*

We put the question 'How do web search engines work?' to AskMe by going through the following procedure:

We entered the search topic 'internet' on the box in the first page (see Figure 6.3). This took us to the 'Enter Your Question' screen (Figure 6.5).

Having entered our query, we were taken to another screen showing various categories. There we were asked to choose a category so that our question could be sent to the right expert. We chose the first option, 'Internet & the Web' (Figure 6.6), and then we were asked to select related activities (Figure 6.7).

AskMe then took us to another page stating that our question had been sent. After a short while (on the same day), we received an e-mail message from AskMe.com stating that our question was answered, and we were given a URL (for AskMe.com) to check the answer. There we received the following answer:

Anonymous asked this question on 3/6/2001:
How do web search engines work?
Merlan gave this response on 3/6/2001:
these seem to me rather good short introductions into 'how web search engines work':
http://www.webreference.com/content/search/
http://www.learnthenet.com/english/animate/search.html

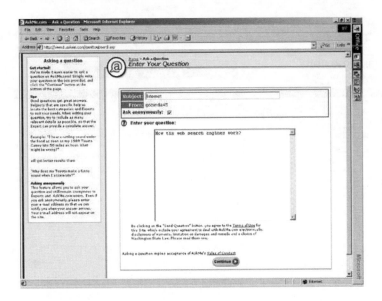

Fig. 6.5   *AskMe 'Enter Your Question' page*

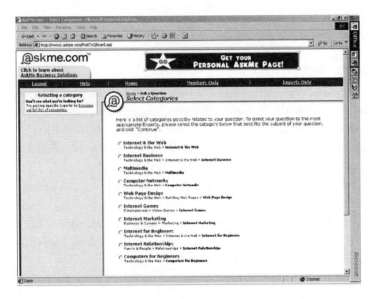

Fig. 6.6   *AskMe 'Select Categories' page*

http://www.mywebteam.com/solutions/5b_searchengine.htm
If you need more detailed information let me know
merlan

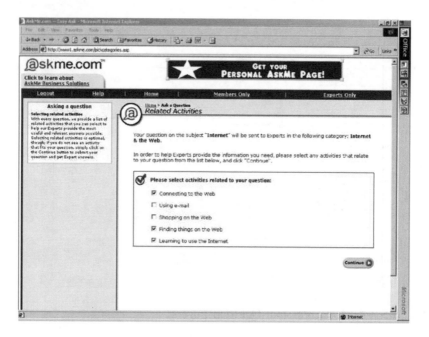

Fig. 6.7 *AskMe 'Related Activities' page*

AllExperts.com

Created in early 1998, AllExperts is a free web-based reference service. A large number of volunteers, including lawyers, doctors, engineers and scientists, answer the questions. All answers are free and most come within a day; the maximum delay in getting an answer could be three days. Figure 6.8 shows the home page, where the user selects a category. Each category has its subcategories, and finally users get a list of experts in a subject area. The user chooses an expert from the list provided, and along with the details of the expert's name, experience, etc., the user gets a rating of his/her performance. This helps the user to select (or reject) an expert. Once the user has selected an expert, he or she enters his or her question (Figure 6.9).

Fig. 6.8   *AllExperts.com home page*

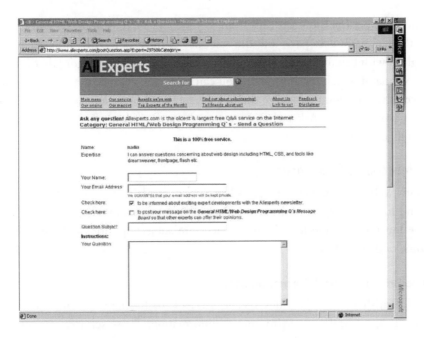

Fig. 6.9   *AllExperts.com 'Question' page*

Inforocket.com

This is a service where users can ask a question which will be answered by experts for a fee. The steps involved in the process are as follows:

1   The user enters a question on the home page with as much detail as possible.
2   He or she indicates how much he or she is willing to pay for an answer by choosing a price range from the drop-down menu.
3   The user enters a contact e-mail address.
4   The user places his or her question in all relevant categories so that the qualified experts can find it and send their offers.
5   After a question is put forward, it is posted on the site and sent out via e-mail to the Inforocket Experts. If one of them knows the answer, the expert sends an offer via Inforocket.com. The offer states the expert's qualifications and the price he or she would like to charge for answering.
6   The user then chooses an expert to answer the question, and selects a payment option. Inforocket then sends the answer to the user, and the user can grade it from a high of 4 to a low of 1. All grades and comments that the user gives and receives are recorded in his or her profile.

The price per question can vary from $5 to $75 or more. Inforocket takes 30% of the fee that a user pays, and the rest goes to the expert. Any individual can register with Inforocket to provide an expert service: 'Find a category that's right for you, and search for a question you can answer. Convince the member who asked the question that you're the best person for the job, and set the price for your answer. If the Asker chooses you and you provide a satisfactory answer, you'll get paid.'

Subject-specific services

Many web-based reference services like this are available, and are setting a new trend for the information industry. Pack (2000) lists many of these. A few are free but most charge fees. Some services are subject-specific, and we discuss some of these below.

The British Library Information Services

The British Library provides special services for business, patent, scientific, technical, medical and environmental information. These services range from answering simple questions to finding answers to complex queries involving online database search, etc. While some of these services are free, for others users need to pay. For example, users can ask simple business questions using a form, and can expect an answer within ten working days. Similarly, users can send e-mail with simple environmental queries and can expect an answer within ten working days. A typical answer in such a case may include:

- a list of bibliographies from a British Library Catalogue literature search, and/or
- a list of organizations to contact for more detailed information, and/or
- information retrieved from internet sources.

Users are not charged for this kind of service. However, for complex queries users need to pay. For example, the British Library provides an STM (Science Technology Medicine) search service for which users need to pay at the following rate:

- £82.00 per hour of staff time divided into 15 minute periods, plus
- costs of online searching, plus
- VAT (Value Added Tax).

As stated in the website, most searches take at least 30 minutes and therefore cost £41.00 for staff time + costs for online searching + VAT. The site also mentions that the average list of references costs £80.00 for medical subjects, and between £100.00 and £150.00 for other subjects. Users are also charged a fee if the results are to be faxed.

In order to obtain an STM search service, the user has to fill in a form that has three parts. In the first part users need to fill in their personal details, etc.; in the second part, they need to enter the query, and in the third part they need to specify their preferred mode of delivery, payment, etc. In the second part, it is possible to enter the detailed specification of the query using Boolean operators and specifying date, language, etc., as limiting factors (see Figure 6.10).

Ask Auntie Nolo

This is an American reference service on the subject of law. There is a list of categories from criminal law to internet law, and the user can browse or search the collection from the home page (see Figure 6.11). This site also provides free access to a digital legal encyclopedia. Users can ask a question from the screen as shown in Figure 6.12.

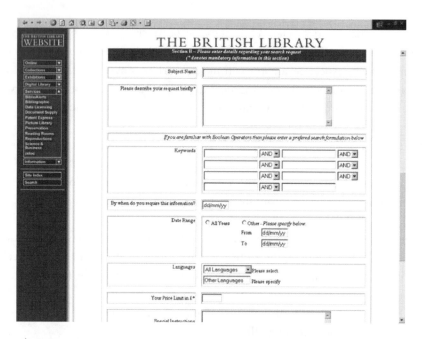

Fig. 6.10 *Section B of the STM Enquiry Form (The British Library STM Search)*

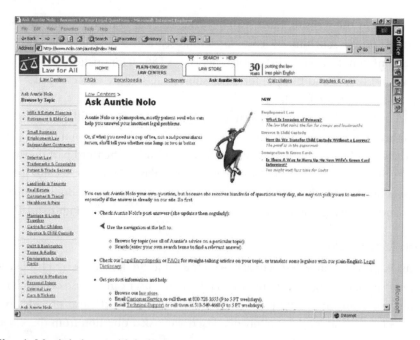

Fig. 6.11 *Ask Auntie Nolo home page*

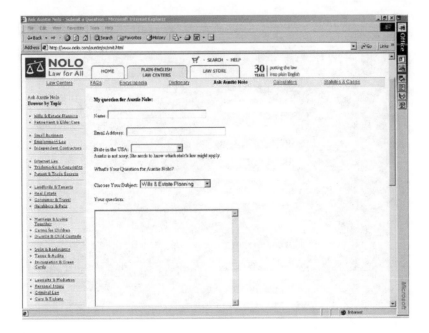

Fig. 6.12 *Ask Auntie Nolo question screen*

FIND/SVP

This is a web-based reference service for business-related queries, and it charges $250 per question. Figures 6.13 and 6.14 show the 'Ask a Question' page. Users need to provide personal details as well as information related to the answer-delivery methods and mode of payment. A question can be on any topic, including a trend, a company, new marketing practices, or industry rumour. Users can take a look at some sample questions and answers. Users are asked to give reasons for asking the question (see Figure 6.14), to specify if there are any geographic or special considerations that need to be addressed, and to mention if they have already done any research on the given topic or question.

Once the question is sent, a consultant will contact the user to discuss his or her specific needs. The expert then begins to search for the required information from in-house subject files and reference and journal collection, the web, online databases and other sources. Finally an answer is provided to the user, usually within two days, by phone, e-mail, fax or courier (as specified by the user). The answer also includes a brief summary with suggestions for next steps, if necessary, accompanied by a dossier of findings as appropriate.

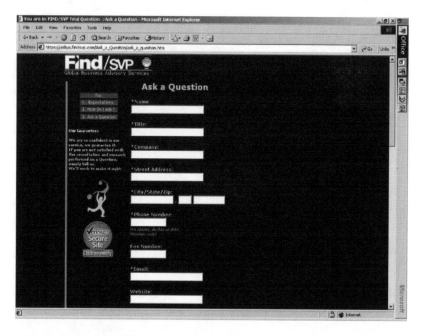

Fig. 6.13 *Find/SVP 'Ask a Question' page (top)*

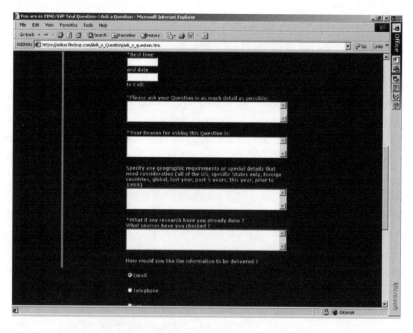

Fig. 6.14 *Find/SVP 'Ask a Question' page (continuation)*

Professional City.com

ProfessionalCity.com provides an information service according to disciplines such as law, accounting, marketing, human resources and information technology. Figure 6.15 shows the ProfessionalCity.com home page. This site also provides access to free and pay-for journals, news services, and other valuable references available online for members of a chosen profession. One of the most interesting services of ProfessionalCity.com is a personalized information service through what it calls a Cybrarian that acts 'as your personal research assistant and will conduct online research on ANY topic you choose'. Figure 6.16 shows the screen where a user can enter a question for the Cybrarian. The answer is usually provided within one business day. This is a fee-based service, and the fee is based on the time spent by the Cybrarian at the rate of $25.00 for the first 15 minutes, with $18.75 per each additional 15-minute increment thereafter.

Web-based reference services where users need to search or browse

Many web-based reference services now exist that allow users to browse or search for the required information and obtain an answer. In this section we shall discuss the features of some of these services.

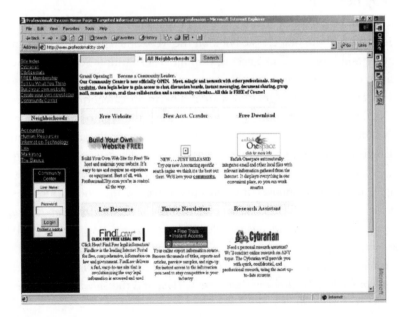

Fig. 6.15 *ProfessionalCity.com home page*

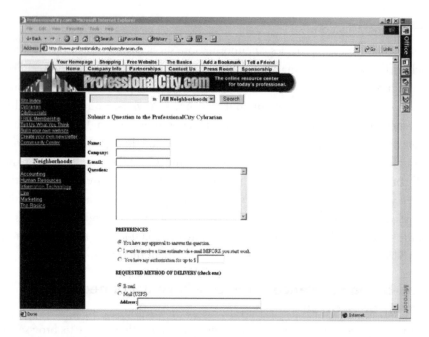

Fig. 6.16 *ProfessionalCity.com question page*

Bartleby Reference

Bartleby.com began as a personal research experiment in 1993, and within one year it published the first classic book on the web. Since then it has grown significantly, and it provides free access, through a very simple search interface, to a number of digital information resources.

Users can select a category to search. The main categories are: reference, verse, fiction and non-fiction. You can also select the type of reference tool to search. The main categories are: encyclopedia, dictionary, thesaurus, quotations, and English usage. When the user selects a particular category, e.g. reference, verse, etc., the list of documents under the category appears on the screen. For example, if the user chooses the reference category, the choice includes the *Columbia encyclopedia* (2001), *The world factbook* (2000), the *American Heritage® dictionary of the English language* (2000), *Roget's II: the new thesaurus* (1995), *Roget's international thesaurus of English words and phrases* (1922) and so on. The verse category contains, among others, *The Oxford book of English verse* (1919), *The Oxford book of English mystical verse* (1917), and the *Yale book of American verse* (1919), and so on.

Users can select any specific item listed, or can conduct a search by entering search terms or phrases in the search box appearing on the top of the page (see Figure 6.17). Search results are arranged in order of relevance (Figure 6.18), and each result provides brief information about the record. Clicking on the result retrieves full information.

Britannica.com

Britannica.com is a free information service on the web that allows the user to search and retrieve information from the *Encyclopedia Britannica*, as well as a number of other web information resources, such as selected articles from more than 70 of the world's top magazines, including Newsweek, Discover, and The Economist. There is also a guide to the web's best sites, covering more than 125,000 sites, and users can search the text of more than 100 million web pages. From the Britannica.com home page you can enter a search expression in the search box (as shown in Figure 6.19), or you can click on a category, such as news, history, science and technology, health, education, etc. Once you have chosen a category, three subcategories appear: Internet Guide, Encyclopedia

Fig. 6.17 *Bartleby.com reference home page*

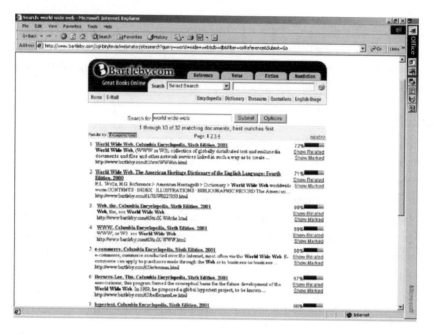

Fig. 6.18 *Results of a search on Bartleby.com*

and Features Archive. You can either enter a search expression after choosing a particular subject category, or can select a subcategory that will lead to a list of relevant topics, with hyperlinks to a subject directory specific to the chosen topic.

Fig. 6.19 *The Britannica.com simple search box*

A search on Britannica.com search brings results in different categories, such as Encyclopaedia Britannica, the web's best sites, magazines, current events and Britannica.com articles, etc. The user can combine search terms using Boolean AND, OR and NOT operators. Plus and minus signs can be used to activate Boolean AND and NOT searches. The operator 'ADJ' can be used between two search terms to conduct a proximity search. An asterisk after a search term is used for truncation, and a phrase can be entered within double quotes. The user can also conduct a natural language search simply by entering a phrase or a sentence.

The advanced search screen of Britannica.com has two parts. The first part allows users to select a particular information source (see Figure 6.20). Once a particular source is selected, the user can then formulate the query in the second part (Figure 6.21). Here the user can enter various search terms or phrases, and in each case can specify whether the term/phrase should be searched in the title or in the entire document (the first box shown in Figure 6.21). In the second box, the user can specify an option from four choices (1) the exact phrase, (2) any of the words, (3) all of the words, or (4) none of the words.

Search in this Information Source:

| Entire Document ▼ |

| Britannica.com
Encyclopedia Britannica
Web's Best Sites
Internet |

Fig. 6.20 *Britannica.com advanced search screen, showing the four information sources to choose from*

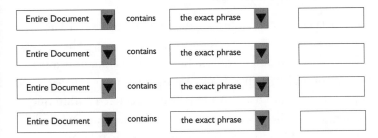

Fig 6.21 *Britannica.com advanced search screen, showing the options for formulating complex search queries*

Electric Library

This is a web-based information service provided by the Infonautics Corporation. This site provides free access to Encyclopedia.com, a digital encyclopedia with more than 50,000 articles. Users can search this encyclopedia or other web resources using a simple search screen (see Figure 6.22). There is also a special information service called the eLibrary Tracker, which searches daily for a particular topic that a user wants, and e-mails the user the latest information. Electric Library offer a ten-day free trial, for which users need to register. The subscription fee is then $59.95 for one year and $99.95 for two years.

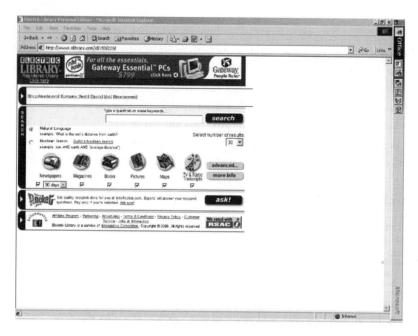

Fig. 6.22 *The Electric Library home page*

At the search screen (Figure 6.22), you can simply enter a natural language query – a phrase or a sentence – and click on the search button. There is also an option for a Boolean search and Advanced Search. You can narrow a search by specifying the type of source, such as books, newspapers, maps, pictures, and so on (see the options on Figure 6.23). A phrase can be entered within quotation marks. By using the advanced search screen, you can narrow any search by publication date, specific author, publication name, or article title. You can set the number of results by selecting 30, 60, 90, 120, or 150 possible documents. You can have your results (Figure 6.24) sorted by relevancy, date, size, reading level, title or publication.

Information Please

Infoplease provides free reference and information services on the web. At this site users can browse and search a wealth of information resources. As shown in Figure 6.25, you can select a specific category, such as sports, entertainment, etc., or can conduct a search on all categories. You then enter a search term or phrase in the search box and click the Go button. A search can be narrowed to specific reference sources. Infoplease conducts searches for all forms of a word: e.g. 'volcano' and 'volcanoes' are considered the same for searching purposes. Phrases

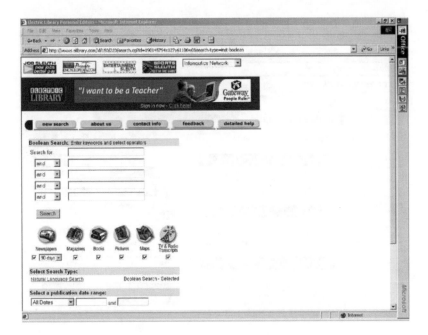

Fig. 6.23 *The Electric Library Boolean search screen*

Fig. 6.24 *Electric Library search results*

Fig. 6.25 *Infoplease.com home page*

are entered in double quotes. Figure 6.26 shows the results of a simple search; users can get the full text by clicking on any item.

Internet Library for Librarians

The Internet Library for Librarians is a free information service provided by the InfoWorks technology Company in the USA. This site provides links to about 3000 sites, each of which has been reviewed by human experts. The information resources are categorized under three main headings:

- ready reference: almanacs, bibliographies, biographies, dictionaries, directories, encyclopedias, maps, etc.
- librarianship: acquisition, automation, cataloguing, reference, etc. and
- accessories: library associations, automated systems, bibliographic utilities, etc.

Users can click on any category to get to the actual resources. For example, when we clicked on Metadata on the home page (Figure 6.27), we got the results shown in Figure 6.28. By clicking on the title on any item in the results page users can go to the actual page of the resource concerned. Users can also

Fig. 6.26 *Infoplease.com search results*

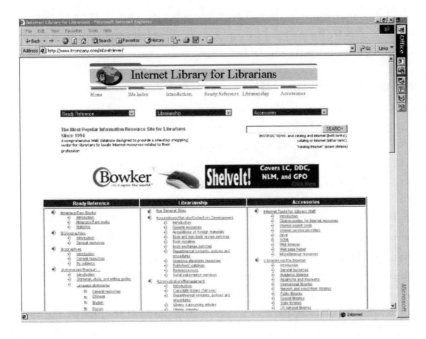

Fig. 6.27 *Internet Library for Librarians home page*

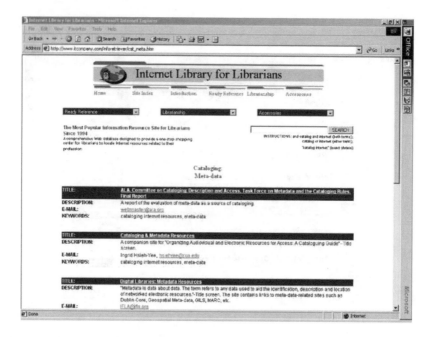

Fig. 6.28 *Internet Library for Librarians search results*

conduct a search from the home page by using search words or phrases. The instructions under the search box (see Figure 6.27) tell users how to conduct an AND, OR and exact phrase searches.

Mediaeater Reference Desk

This is a free web-based reference service available from Mediaeater Inc. The site lists a number of links to online reference sources, as shown in Figure 6.29. Users can click on any link to move to the site and search and/or browse for information. There are links to various dictionaries, encyclopedias, reference works, web tools, translation services, library catalogues, databases and so on.

Research-It!

This is a web-based reference service available from iTools Inc. This site contains several language resources, dictionaries and translation tools, biographical and quotation resources, maps, etc. The major reference categories are language, library, geographical, financial, shipping, and the internet. For each category, on the same page, there is a search box, along with a list of the specific tools available for that category. For example, if users want to use the language tools, then they can use the search box shown in Figure 6.30. They can choose

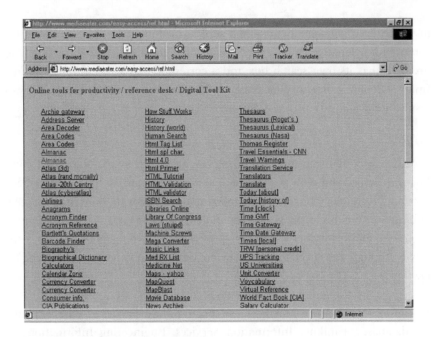

Fig. 6.29 *Mediaeater Reference Desk*

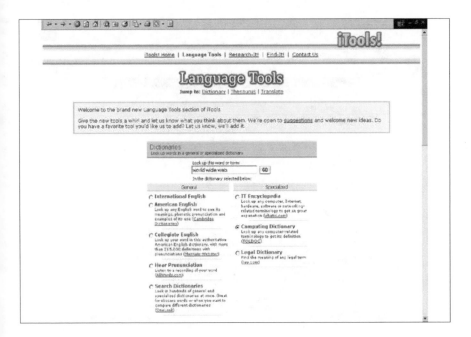

Fig. 6.30 *Research-It! search page (language tools)*

to search in a language dictionary, a subject dictionary, or a thesaurus, or can use an online language translator. Similarly, the geographical tools section (Figure 6.31) has its own search box and a corresponding set of online resources (maps, telephone directory, factbook). When a search is conducted, the relevant results are displayed.

TiARA

TiARA (see p. 81) is an information service developed by the National Library Board in association with the National Computer Board and the National Science and Technology Board of Singapore. It aims to provide a one-stop source of information for the business people, students, parents and teachers, scientists, engineers, and researchers and other professionals in Singapore. This is a free service, though users need to register before use. TiARA's services include the following:

*   information services, including access to online databases, such as Dialog databases, Faulkner Information Services, Engineering Information's Ei

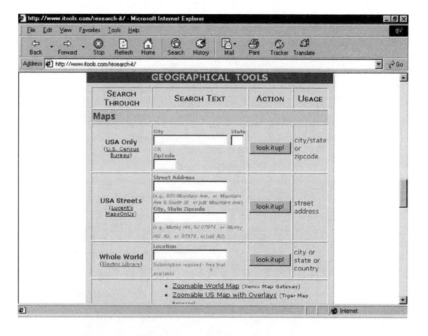

Fig. 6.31 *Research-It! search page (geographical tools)*

Compendex Plus, and Gartner Interactive IT Journal & Business Technology Journal.

- internet resources, a select list of websites that have been reviewed and categorized. Users are welcome to suggest websites for inclusion in the list.
- AskTiARA, an e-mail reference service (see p. 81).

Summary

Although online reference services existed before the arrival of the internet, many more have appeared over recent years. Some are provided by libraries, but many commercial organizations have also begun to provide web-based reference services. Many of these services are free, and experts work voluntarily to search for and answer reference queries. Many services are also provided in specific subject fields. Some services charge users as much as $250 per question. There are also online reference services that allow users to browse and search many electronic reference sources. These web-based reference and information services are a great asset to end-users, who can now access information on specific topics from their desk, and in most cases it is free.

These services have also brought two significant changes in the information industry. First, reference and information services are no longer seen as the exclusive remit of library and information professionals; reference services are now provided by many subject experts through the internet. Second, reference services were once very costly, since they involved expensive reference tools and also the valuable time of reference librarians. But this is no longer the case, since many of these tools, in their most up-to-date versions, are now available free, and users do not need to ask a specific reference librarian for help; they can find information on their own, or can look for experts across the web who are willing to offer free help.

Chapter 7
Electronic journals

Introduction

The term electronic journal can mean many things, ranging from a distribution format for a print journal, an electronic archive of a print journal to a journal published exclusively in an electronic format (Fecko, 1997; Jones, 1999). Lancaster (1995) suggests that an electronic journal is created for the electronic medium and is available only in this medium. According to Jones (1998), although people use different names for electronic journals it is a fact that 'they are available electronically via a computer or a computer network, that they may or may not be published in some other (physical) medium, but that they are not CD-ROMs or diskettes'. Jones further notes that people call these publications by a variety of names, such as ejournals, e-journals, electronic journals, eserials, e-serials, electronic serials, e-zines, internet-based electronic journals, internet-based serials, on-line journals, and so on. However, over the years, the term 'e-journal' has become more popular than the others. In fact, a quick search of the LISA Plus CD-ROM database in August 2000, using the keyword search facility, retrieved 6 records on 'e-zine$', 7 records on 'ejournal$', 690 records on 'e-serial$', and 3624 records on 'e-journal$'.

The salient features of e-journals can be summarized as follows (Fecko, 1997; Electronic journals, n.d.):

- they can be delivered to the desktop
- they can be read by more than one person at a time
- the text can be searched
- they can include multimedia and graphics, in colour, at marginal cost

- they can be published more quickly than paper publications
- they can be interactive; they can foster an online exchange of ideas by e-mail
- they can make use of hyperlinks, both internally and to other publications
- articles can be retrieved directly through links from abstracting and indexing databases
- the content can be reproduced, forwarded, and modified, leading to possible problems with copyright protection and preserving authenticity.

The main disadvantage of e-journals is that, unless they are also printed on paper, they require specialized equipment for reading. Another possible disadvantage is that libraries and users do not own the journals; they obtain an access right for a specific period of time.

In recent years there has been a rapid increase in the number of e-journals, and they now form a significant part of any library's collection. Various sources chart the growth of electronic journals. From 1991 to 1997, the Association of Research Libraries (ARL; see p. 124) followed the growth of electronic publications through its annual *Directory of electronic journals, newsletters and academic discussion lists* (Mogge, 1999). In the early 1990s e-journals were edited and published by scholars and academics on a voluntary basis. Mainly humanities and social science subject areas were covered. Most of these publications were available through either FTP sites or e-mail using listserv software. The web has facilitated the growth and accessibility of e-journals.

Many e-journals began as experimental ventures which subsequently became permanent. For example, Project MUSE (see p. 117) began as a collaboration between the library and university press at Johns Hopkins University (JHU) in 1993. It now offers institutional access to over 100 e-journals in the humanities, social science and mathematics (Project MUSE). The dramatic rise in both peer-reviewed and fee-based e-journals in 1996 and 1997 is accounted for by large publishers such as Academic Press, Chapman-Hall, Elsevier, and Springer offering many, if not all, of their print products online (Mogge, 1999). Many sources now provide lists of e-journals that are available: see, for example, the ARL *Directory of scholarly electronic journals and academic discussion lists* (ARL, n.d.).

Nowadays there are two major categories of e-journals: those that have their printed counterparts, for example, the *Journal of Documentation*, and those that are available only in electronic format, for example, *D-Lib Magazine*. Several authors have discussed how electronic journals are used by various categories of users: see, for example, McKnight (1997); Neal (1997) and Miller (1999).

Access to e-journals

In order to make the optimum use of e-journals one needs to access, browse and/or search them in the most convenient way. Users need access to the appropriate IT – computers and communication facilities. In addition, users need to learn the techniques of using e-journals. In this chapter we shall discuss these techniques, and how they differ from one system to another.

There are many issues for libraries to consider: technology requirements, restricted access, access via publisher or aggregator, and making library patrons aware of online access. Several authors discuss the primary formats used by electronic journal providers: HTML, Adobe Acrobat PDF (portable document format), and the increasing importance of SGML (standardized genneneralized markup language). Machovec (1997); Porteous (1997); Hudson and Windsor (1998); Luther (1998) and Schoonbaert (1998) review the enhanced features of online journal access provided through web technology, such as hyperlinks to related texts and links to multimedia.

Access to electronic journals is provided either by publishers themselves or aggregators. Most e-journal publishers provide access to their journals from their websites (Lee and Morris, 2000). Usually if a library subscribes to the print version of a journal, access to its electronic version is available free or for a small additional fee. To save libraries the inconvenience of dealing with a variety of e-journal publishers, organizations known as aggregators have started services that provide access to more than one e-journal. These can be subscription agents, database providers, index and abstract publishers, or primary publishers (McKay, 1999), and they organize e-journal access, and administer passwords, table of content services, usage statistics and archiving (Lee and Morris, 2000). They also offer the advantage of providing access to a number of e-journals through one search interface.

The benefits of getting direct access to an individual publisher's journals are value-added features and lack of intermediaries. Aggregators, on the other hand, conglomerate journals of several publishers under one interface and search system. Machovec (1997) and Luther (1998) list major publishers and aggregators with details on their products, formats used, special features, and collaborations with other online products. Schoonbaert (1998) provides a list of URLs for publishers and aggregators, such as, Blackwell's Electronic Journal Navigator, Swetsnet, EBSCO Online, and so on.

Aggregators

There are many aggregators providung access to various different journals. They differ in the search and browse features that they offer. The following are some popular aggregators.

Blackwell's Electronic Journal Navigator is designed to offer a single point of access, reference, control and financial management for a library's electronic journal subscription. Blackwell's does not archive journals but provides an interface to many different titles with different publishers on the internet, and it acts as a full service subscription agent for centralized ordering, consolidating invoicing and a central point for administration. This is a subscription-based electronic journal aggregator providing access to 1925 journals. Users can log in in two ways: either directly through the IP address arranged by the library with Blackwell, or by entering the user name and password in the relevant fields.

DirectLink provides URL links into Electronic Journal Navigator (EJN) at journal issue level for a specific journal. There is a DirectLink URL for each journal available on EJN. When a user clicks on a link in the OPAC (online public access catalogue) or on the library web page (using DirectLink), the EJN log-in page opens for authentication. A list of journal issues is then presented. (To set up the DirectLink first, go to the URL **http://search.navigator.blackwell.co.uk/ Pages/jnl_urls.txt**; an alphabetical list and their associated links will appear; copy the DirectLink URL of the chosen journal and paste the URL into the desired location in the web page.)

Major features of EJN include the following (Harrassowitz, n.d.):

- Journal Search and Whole File Search are available to subscribers only
- over 1900 journals are covered
- full text is available in two formats – PDF and RealPage
- individual electronic articles cannot be purchased by non-members
- it works with standard web browsers and offers a search engine to search abstracts and citation information
- it offers an alerting service to keep users aware of new issues of selected key journals that have been published and added to the website
- a transactional (i.e. pay per view) delivery of articles is also offered: therefore, if a library does not subscribe to a particular e-journal title, the user may pay for a single viewing of an article.

SwetsnetNavigator (Figure 7.1) provides a comprehensive source for electronic titles, with 5130 titles from 147 publishers currently available. It also offers a single point of access to a large and growing range of full-text titles as well as table of contents and abstracts. Blackwell's Information Services and Swets Subscription Service officially merged in 2000, in which year their electronic journal services were integrated (Harrassowitz, n.d.)

The major features of SwetsnetNavigator include the following:

- access to full-text articles is provided to authorized subscribers
- there are over 16,000 journals with tables of contents (TOCs)
- users can search the library's own subscriptions, individual/departmental collections as well as the entire SwetsnetNavigator database
- selective dissemination of information (SDI) and table of contents notification are available
- full text is available in two formats – PDF and RealPage
- Journal Search allows users to search in specific fields
- Whole File Search allows users to search table of contents information, abstracts, and other fields

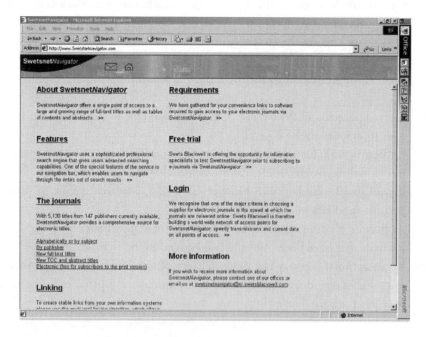

Fig. 7.1   *The SwetsnetNavigator home page*

- an article alert service, speedy delivery and 24 hour global connectivity, title history and review indicators are also available
- individual electronic article cannot be purchased by non-members.

Users can search in a defined set (meaning they can select any of these options: all journals, all full-text journals, all abstract journals, new journals, free electronic journals) and journal subject (they can select all subjects, social sciences, religion, arts, medicine, etc.), and can specify the search term in the proposed field. The journals can be searched by subject or can be browsed alphabetically, by publishers, by new full-text titles, by new TOC and abstract titles, and by electronic free journals (free for subscribers to the print version).

Figure 7.2 shows the screen that allows a user to browse titles alphabetically. The user can select a subject from a drop-down list, or can enter a search term in the search box, to obtain a list of journals in the chosen subject or topic. Similar screens are available for the other options.

EBSCO Online is an aggregator that provides access to full-text articles from over 4000 scholarly journals, containing over 1 million full-text articles. Figure 7.3 shows the EBSCO online home page. As the figure indicates, users can

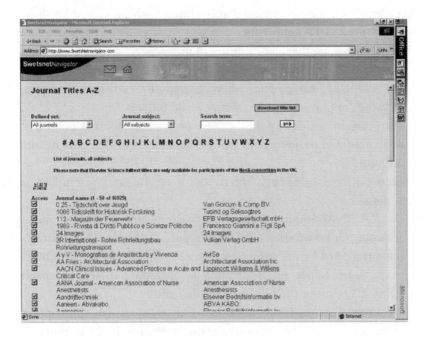

Fig. 7.2 *SwetsnetNavigator search screen*

Fig. 7.3   *The EBSCO Online home page*

select a server on the global map that is nearest to them. Figure 7.4 shows the
EBSCO Online (UK) home page.

The following are the major features of the service:

- the ARTICLESearch option allows users to find articles by searching for
  keywords or phrases in titles, abstracts and full text
- users can also search by publisher keywords, author, journal, publisher, year
  or a range of years, journal volume and number, and even titles not on subscription
- users can save their search criteria and reuse the saved search later in the
  session
- the JOURNALSearch option allows users to find electronic journals by
  searching for keywords in titles, ISSNs, publisher names or content descriptions (supplied by the publisher). Searches can be expanded to find electronic journals not on subscription by including all titles available via
  EBSCO Online or through the publisher site
- the Browse option allows users to see a list of current subscriptions, or
  expand a search to include other electronic journals available from publishers

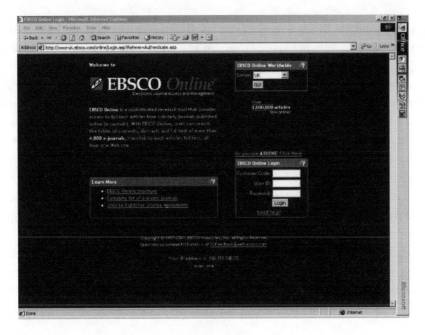

Fig. 7.4   *The EBSCO Online (UK) home page*

- users can view LC subject codes and descriptions assigned to each journal. They will also have the option of selecting a subject for which they can retrieve a list of all related journals
- full text is available in three formats – PDF, HTML and RealPage
- EBSCO Online access is granted only to organizations, such as libraries and their patrons, not to individuals.

Ingenta is the global research gateway designed to serve the various online information needs of users. Since its inception in 1998, it has grown significantly, and currently offers a number of services, such as:

- free access to article summaries: the website currently shows that it provides access to 10,636,853 articles from 24,477 publications
- access to the full texts of articles which is available to registered users or on a pay-per-view basis
- access to the MEDLINE database
- facilities for browsing journals by subject and by publishers
- delivery of full text articles online or by fax
- facilities for setting up personal profiles of users.

For accessing the Ingenta services one usually does not need to register. In fact anyone can use Ingenta and can, where available, access the summary of any article. However, by registering with Ingenta, users can access the full-text of their own, or their institutional, subscriptions and can set up a personal profile. However, even if the user does not register, they can get full texts on a pay-per-view basis. Ingenta also provides a range of free and customized online services to libraries, such as campus-wide access to subscribed full text articles, and other facilities for library management.

On the first screen of Ingenta (Figure 7.5) users can do a quick search for articles in the Ingenta collection, search MEDLINE, select a particular subject field from a list, or choose to browse publications by selecting the 'Browse Publications' link. Figure 7.6 shows the search screen of Ingenta.

The search screen allows users to further search MEDLINE and the Ingenta collection. Users are allowed to create a personal profile for the Ingenta services, and saved searches can be retrieved through the search screen (Figure 7.6). After a search is conducted, users can:

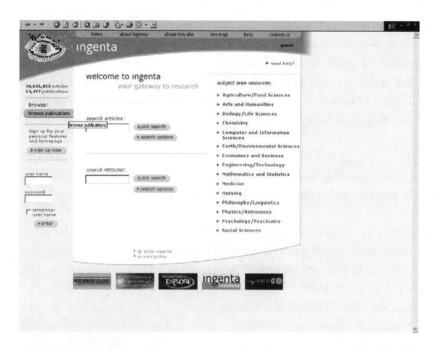

Fig. 7.5 *Ingenta home page*

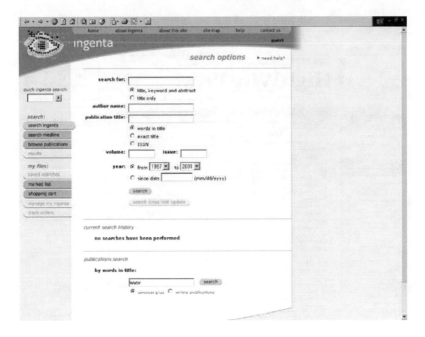

Fig. 7.6 *Ingenta advanced search screen*

- view the article summary
- create a marked list of articles that can be downloaded or emailed
- view the full text if they or their institution is a registered subscriber
- purchase the article by adding it to their shopping cart, if they are not registered subscribers.

Electronic journal publishers (projects)

A number of projects began in the nineties with a view to publishing e-journals. Those involved were not traditional commercial publishers. Their objective was to make e-journals easily available to libraries and users at an affordable price. In this section we shall discuss some of these projects.

HighWire Press

Stanford University Library's HighWire Press (Figure 7.7) began in early 1995 with the online production of the weekly *Journal of Biological Chemistry* (*JBC*). By March 2001, HighWire was producing 240 online journals giving access to 237,711 articles. The journals focus on science, technology and medicine, and are the highest-impact journals in the literature. HighWire's approach to online

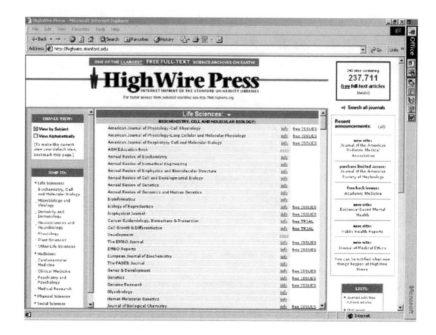

Fig. 7.7 *The HighWire Press home page*

publishing of scholarly journals is not simply to mount electronic images of printed pages; rather, by adding links among authors, articles and citations, advanced searching capabilities, high-resolution images and multimedia, and interactivity, the electronic versions provide added dimensions to the information provided in the printed journals.

The major features of HighWire Press include the following:

- each journal has its own URL domain; HighWire acts as host for Science, Proceedings of the National Academy of Sciences, Oxford University Press, American Society for Microbiology, Annual Reviews, etc.
- Journal Search is open to non-subscribers
- to get the best search results, information such as volume/page number, author(s), and/or specific keywords should be given
- search results can be displayed according to relevance
- phrases, wild cards, Boolean logic, stemming, etc. can be used
- full-text searches can identify a valuable range of articles, such as articles from a specific institution, articles using a special technique, etc.
- full-text documents are available in PDF and HTML formats

- individual electronic articles can be purchased by non-members (selected journals only)
- table of contents notification is available for which no subscription is required.

JSTOR

JSTOR was established as an independent not-for-profit organization in August 1995, with the objective to ease the increasing problems faced by libraries seeking to provide adequate stack space for the long runs of backfiles of scholarly journals. It began as a pilot project to provide electronic access to the backfiles of ten journals in two core fields, economics and history. Currently JSTOR covers various disciplines including, arts and sciences, general science, and ecology and botany. Access to the full JSTOR database is available only through affiliation with a participating institution or through an account with a participating publisher. Access from on-campus is determined either by IP addresses provided by participating sites, or via ATHENS for affiliates of participating UK and Ireland sites.

The following are the major features of JSTOR:

- users can search or browse the collection
- Whole File Search allows users to search specific fields, such as title, abstract, author, full text, journal categories, and date range
- full text is available in different PDF and PostScript formats
- individual electronic articles cannot be purchased by non-members
- the collection is mainly archival; individuals can subscribe to certain journals.

Project MUSE

Project MUSE provides access to over 100 e-journals covering the fields of literature and criticism, history, the visual and performing arts, cultural studies, education, political science, gender studies, and many others. Subscriptions are available only to institutions, but when a library subscribes, the database is made available to the entire campus, not just workstations at the library. Using any web browser, faculty, students, staff and library patrons of subscribing institutions can view and search the database from wherever they are on campus without the need for passwords.

The following are the major features of Project MUSE:

- users can perform keyword and Boolean searches
- full-text searches can be conducted across all journals in the database, selected journal titles, or in just a single title
- users can search tables of contents of articles and book reviews by author and title, as well as by Library of Congress subject headings
- page numbers from the print edition are embedded in the electronic text for easy citation and referencing
- illustrations are larger and sharper than those in the print journal
- images can be displayed in four sizes
- Library of Congress subject headings following each article title in the tables of contents and embedded in article files can be used for accurate searching
- unlimited downloading and printing facilities are available to members of the subscribing institutions
- the electronic version of journals is available earlier than the print edition.

Electronic journal publishers

Some commercial publishers provide access to their own journals. Each of these publishers has its own search interface, through which all its titles can be accessed. Features of some e-journal publishers and their search interfaces are discussed below.

IDEAL

IDEAL (the International Digital Electronic Access Library) is the online journal library from Academic Press. It now contains over 200,000 articles from nearly 250 journals, covering science, technology and medicine. Figure 7.8 shows the IDEAL home page, Figure 7.9 shows the search screen and Figure 7.10 shows the browse screen.

The following are the major features of IDEAL:

- journals can be browsed by title (alphabetically), by subject category, and by publisher.
- Journal Page displays the current issue's table of contents. The user may navigate to any abstract in this issue by clicking the 'Abstract' link of the article that the user wishes to view

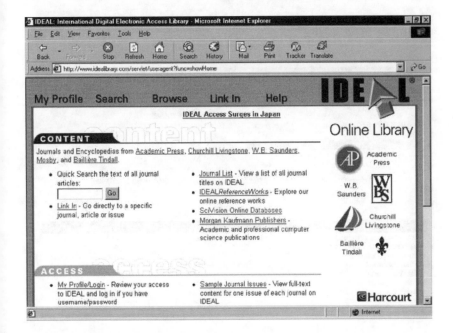

Fig. 7.8 *The IDEAL home page*

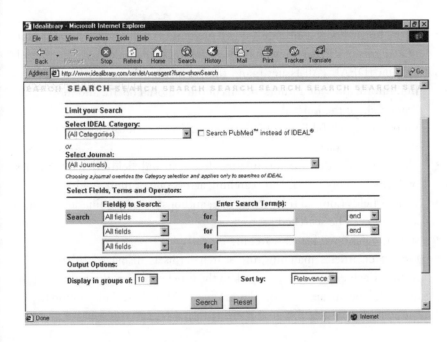

Fig. 7.9 *The IDEAL search screen*

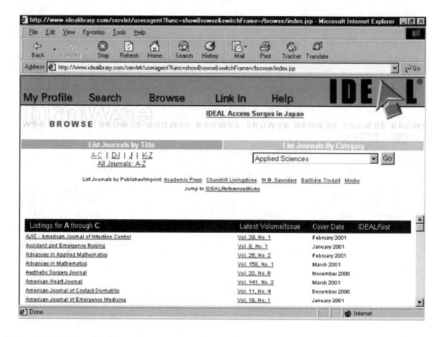

Fig. 7.10 *The IDEAL browse screen*

- in the Journal Navigation pull-down menu users will find links to the table of contents of the two previous issues, the full listing of all the issues available on IDEAL ('All Issues'), and the journal home page, where you can find information for authors, details of the editorial board, and more information about the journal
- users can search bibliographic (article header or citation) information and the article abstracts
- forms are provided for formulating free-text and field-oriented queries, with Boolean operators, and searching across one or more fields
- various fields (journal title, article title, author surname, affiliation, abstract and date) can be searched
- stemming and wild-card searching is available
- the list of articles matching the search terms is displayed in the search results. Each entry includes a link to the article abstract, the full text of the article (if you are an authorized user), and a 'More Like This' option to perform another search.

ScienceDirect

Elsevier's ScienceDirect offers access to over 1200 journals and navigation across 30 million records with links to 10,000 journal titles. ScienceDirect is designed to serve the research needs of academic, corporate and educational institutions, by offering comprehensive coverage in all scientific fields. The full-text collection of over 1 million articles from 1995 to the present covers subject areas and disciplines including: biochemistry, biological sciences, business and management science, chemistry, clinical medicine, earth sciences, economics, engineering and technology, environmental science, materials science, mathematics and computer science, microbiology and immunology, neurosciences, pharmacology and toxicology, physics and social sciences.

The following are the major features of ScienceDirect:

- journals can be browsed by title, subject, publisher or issue. Users can browse tables of contents for recently published articles or go directly to full text
- personalized features include: journal lists, e-mail alerts and saved searches
- a search can be executed across the abstracts database containing over 1.8 million abstracts from the core journals in the major scientific disciplines, and all Elsevier Science abstracts
- the View Abstracts option is available for all titles in ScienceDirect, even for journals to which the user's institution does not subscribe. If the full text of the journal article is not available, the user may order the article through document delivery
- a search can be conducted in specific fields, such as title, abstract, keywords, author, full text, references, subject categories, date, volume, issue, and page
- full-text article access is available for over 1200 Elsevier Science journals, as well as 100 titles from participating publishers who have their content on the ScienceDirect platform
- full text is available in PDF and (for some titles) in HTML format
- there are two search options: Basic Search for the novice researcher, and Enhanced Search, which provides powerful proximity and Boolean search facilities
- search forms are tailored to content type, journals, abstracts, journals and abstracts, or reference works
- retrospective searching of valuable older material provides a comprehensive overview of the research literature
- cross-database searching allows seamless searching across all or a selected

abstract database to enhance retrieval of research literature from all sources
- SummaryPlus is a feature that allows users to determine quickly whether the article fits their research needs.

D-Lib

D-Lib offers facilities to browse, access and comment on current work in digital library research, advanced development and implementation. The journal facilitates communication among the many agencies, organizations, institutions, and individuals participating or interested in digital library research and its eventual application. The magazine disseminates descriptions of current research and implementation projects, and provides for interaction with the community through announcements and communications to the Editor. Figure 7.11 shows the D-Lib home page, and Figure 7.12 shows the search screen.

The following are the major features of D-Lib:

- users can browse by title, author or by back issues; back issues can also be browsed by content pages, keyword/concepts, author index, title index, or monthly issues
- matching can be set so that the search results match all of the terms in the search string, any of the terms, or two or more terms combined with Boolean logic
- the Short format displays only a list of titles, the Long format displays titles, plus an excerpt showing the search string in its context, from either the contents of the meta tag, an extract of text containing the search word, or the initial text on the page
- search results can be sorted by score (relevance), time (by date they were last updated), and by title (alphabetically). The sort orders may be reversed
- searching is case-insensitive
- each page is given a rating of one to five stars
- the present version of the search engine software only allows for searching on words rather than complete phrases.

Identification tools

A number of directories and guides have been prepared by professionals for identification of e-journals. Some of these are described below.

Fig. 7.11 *D-Lib Magazine home page*

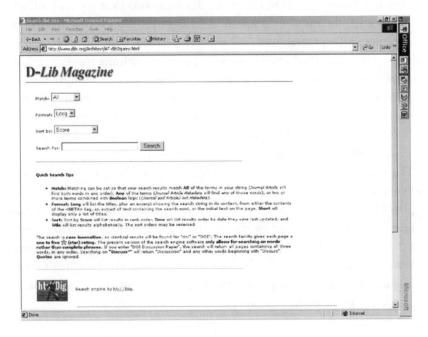

Fig. 7.12 *D-Lib Magazine search screen*

BUBL Journals

All information in BUBL Journals is freely available to all users without registration and without the need for any software other than a web browser. Since BUBL began in 1990, an important part of its service has been the provision of electronic newsletters, journals, abstracts, and tables of contents. These have now been brought together into the distinct BUBL Journals service. The content is organized such that all titles that are no longer issued or no longer received by BUBL are stored in the BUBL Archive. This leaves a total of over 200 current titles which have abstracts and tables of contents stored in BUBL Journals. About two-thirds of these relate to library and information science. There is also reasonable coverage of titles covering social, medical and business topics. Not all titles are refereed academic journals, as BUBL Journals also holds contents and abstracts from a selection of newsletters and magazines.

ARL Directory

The ARL *Directory of scholarly electronic and academic discussion lists* (web version) lists electronic journals and newsletters as well as thousands of scholarly listservs. ARL is a not-for-profit membership organization comprising the leading research libraries in North America. Its mission is to shape and influence forces affecting the future of research libraries in the process of scholarly communication. ARL programmes and services promote equitable access to and effective use of recorded knowledge in support of teaching, research, scholarship, and community service. In addition to offering a single resource for locating electronic serials, a primary benefit of the ARL *Directory* has been the vetting done on each title it contains. Users can search for an individual title by various means, as well as link directly to the e-journal website. The ARL *Directory* was published originally in *Library Hi Tech* (ARL, 1999).

The online version of the *Directory* offers users the ability to browse through individual entries or to search for specific items. Search options include searching by title, description, publisher, peer review basis, or subject. Also included online is the thesaurus used to classify the entries, thereby allowing users to search by specific keywords. All web-accessible e-journals have a link from the *Directory* entry to the journal's own site. The electronic version of the *Directory* is available as a stand-alone product, while purchasers of print copies automatically receive access to the e-version.

The IPL (Internet Public Library) Reading Room Serials Collection
This contains over 3000 titles that can be searched or browsed by subject (such as arts and humanities, business and economics, internet and computers, education, entertainment and leisure, health and medical sciences, law, government and political sciences, and so on) or by title. Newspapers can now be found in a separate section.

Net.Journal Directory
This printed directory is a detailed guide to serials on the web. It helps to find out: where full-text journals are available, how much articles cost, what years are covered, and whether pictures and charts are available for immediate download, and in what format. The twice-yearly directory has over 60,000 listings for more than 15,000 full-text journal and newspaper titles available from both free and fee-based websites and services. Systems covered include DialogWeb, Wilson Web, OCLC's Electronic Collection Online, the Electric Library, Lexis-Nexis Universe, Chemport, OCLC's FirstSearch and Northern Light and John Wiley.

Electronic books

An electronic book (eBook, ebook or e-book), according to Hardin (n.d.), refers to a book sold on floppy disk, CD-ROM, or downloaded from a site. The major characteristics of e-books are:

- they can be delivered instantly
- they are portable, when used with e-book reading machines or laptops
- they are searchable, and hyperlinks and cut-and-paste facilities give them added value
- users can view images, graphics and multimedia
- they do not deteriorate physically over time, as happens with poor quality paper and printing.

We have already discussed several examples of e-books that are the electronic versions of printed books, such as dictionaries, encyclopedias, thesauri, almanacs, and so on, that are accessible through various websites. Many electronic books are accessible through digital libraries (Chapter 8).

A more recent development is the type of e-books that are published exclusively in electronic formats. Special software or a specially designed device is needed to read these. Many tools for reading eBooks are now available, of which some are commercial products, some are available free, and some are still at an experimental or prototype stage. Examples of these products are given by Hardin (n.d.), and at the Webopedia, Barnes & Noble and eBooks websites: Rocket eBook,from Nuvomedia, SoftBook from SoftBook Press, Microsoft Reader from Microsoft, RCA eBook, Adobe Acrobat Ebook Reader, Everybook, Inc.'s Everybook Dedicated Reader™, DEC Lectrice Virtual Book, Librius' Millennium Ebook, Acorn NewsPad, MIT Media Lab's Victorian Laptop, Anigma WebMan®, Cyrix WebPad™ and FXPAL's XLibris™.

The producers of e-book readers provide lists of books that are available for purchase and can be read using those tools. Features of three e-book readers are briefly described in the Barnes & Noble web page (Barnes & Noble). Table 7.1 shows these features in brief.

- the Microsoft Reader, software that can be downloaded free
- the RCA REB, a portable, dedicated device for reading e-books, and
- the Adobe Acrobat eBook Reader, software that can be downloaded free.

A variety of e-books can be downloaded from the same site (Figure 7.13).

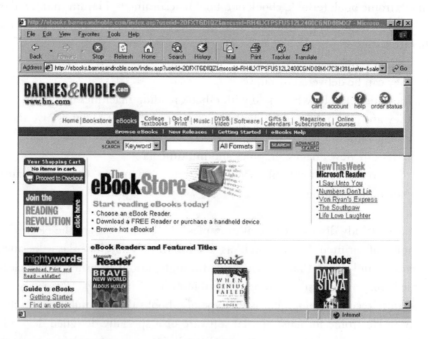

Fig. 7.13 *The Barnes & Noble e-books page*

Table 7.1 Features of e-book Readers

Microsoft Reader	RCA eBook Reader (RCA REB 1100)	Adobe Acrobat eBook Reader
The software is available free; a computer is required	It is a handheld device costing $299; no computer is required	The software is available free; a computer is required
Full colour is available	The screen is monochromatic	Full colour is available
Users can adjust the size of the font and personalize the 'ClearType' to suit the reader's eyes	Users can change the font size as well as the orientation of the text	Users can zoom in and out to suit their needs and 'sharpen' the text. They can also change the orientation of the text.
There is no limit to the number of eBooks that can be held. However, to minimize the space the eBooks take up on the hard drive, users should only download eBooks they are reading and store the rest online in their Microsoft eBook Account.	It can hold approximately ten eBooks	The only limitation is the space each eBook takes up on the user's hard drive
Allows users to • Take Notes • Highlight Text • Find Words/Phrases • Create Drawings • Bookmark	Allows users to • Make notes in the margins • Highlight Text • Find words/phrases • Free interactive dictionary • Bookmark • Backlit Screen	Allows users to • Bookmark • Find words/phrases • High-quality graphics • Take notes • Two-page view • Spoken text (with the publisher's permission)

Summary

Electronic journals and electronic books have brought significant developments in the information industry. They are easy to deliver to users in terms of time and space, but pose different types of access and collection management problems. Nevertheless, users can easily browse and search electronic journals and books, and thus can make better use of the information contained in these publications. However, the search interfaces provided by journal publishers and aggregators vary significantly, and users need to learn the various search skills to make optimum use of them. The same is true of e-books. While the electronic versions of journals and books are opening up more opportunities for end-users, they also require users to be skilled in the information search and retrieval process.

Chapter 8
Digital libraries

Introduction

Recent developments in information technology, the internet and world wide web, coupled with increased funding for research on the creation, access and management of electronic information resources, have led to the development of the new era of electronic or digital libraries. Considerable amounts of money have been allocated to digital library research, and a large number of researchers are working all over the world. In the United States $24 million was awarded in 1994 as part of the first Digital Library Initiative (DLI-1), and about $44 million was allocated for the second phase (DLI-2) (Fox, 1999; Griffin, 1999). Other research projects on digital libraries are reported by Chowdhury and Chowdhury (1999) and Arms (2000). Research in the United Kingdom has largely been funded by the Electronic Libraries Programme, eLib. The first two phases of eLib cost £15 million over three years; in this period JISC spent about £24 million on data services and probably £50 million on networks (Rusbridge, 1998). The third and ongoing phase of eLib (see the eLib website) has sponsored five hybrid library research projects (Pinfield et al., 1998; Rusbridge, 1998).

Lesk (1997, 1999); Raitt (1999) and Arms (2000) have discussed various issues related to research and development in digital libraries. Chowdhury and Chowdhury (1999) reviewed digital library research around the world, and trends in this field were also reported in a special issue of *Information Processing and Management* (Marchionini and Fox, 1999). Regular research in digital libraries is reported in online journals such as *D-Lib Magazine* and *Ariadne* and in other professional journals, printed as well as electronic; at various conferences, such as the ACM Digital Library Conference, European Digital Library Conference, Asian Digital Library Conference, and so on; and also in a number of institutional and personal websites.

Definition and characteristics of a digital library

In the literature the terms digital library and electronic library are used interchangeably, though the latter is more popular in the UK (Chowdhury and Chowdhury, 1999). Borgman (1999) has analysed the various definitions and connotations of digital libraries that have been proposed by researchers throughout the world. She argues that the research community's definition of digital libraries has evolved from a narrower view emphasizing technologies to a broader view encompassing the social, behavioural and economic contexts in which digital libraries are used. In her opinion, the views of the library community are reflected in the definition given by the Digital Library Federation (DLF) as reported by Waters (1998): 'Digital libraries are organizations that provide the resources, including the specialized staff, to select, structure, offer intellectual access to, interpret, distribute, preserve the integrity of, and ensure the persistence over time of collections of digital works so that they are readily and economically available for use by a defined community or set of communities'.

In addition, a new concept, the hybrid library, has also emerged (Pinfield et al., 1998; Rusbridge, 1998; Chowdhury and Chowdhury, 1999; Oppenheim and Smithson, 1999). Rusbridge (1998) suggests that a hybrid library brings a range of technologies from different sources together, and it integrates systems and services in both the electronic and print environments. He further argues that 'the name hybrid library is intended to reflect the transitional state of the library, which today can neither be fully print nor fully digital'. Pinfield et al. (1998) suggest that the hybrid library is on the continuum between the conventional and digital library.

The type of information that a digital library handles ranges from text, numerical data, figures, photographs, maps, slides, to music, video and films. Digital libraries differ from traditional libraries in particular ways, and many publications have discussed these characteristics (Gladney et al., 1994; Vicki and Winograd, 1995; Chowdhury and Chowdhury, 1999). Some of these important characteristics are:

- information resources can vary from simple text to multimedia available at one or several locations; they may be available on different platforms, and may have been created and/or organized differently

- information may come from various sources – from electronic journal producers or vendors to databases; from local digital libraries to remote digital libraries; and so on
- digital materials often form part of a larger collection that comprises print materials
- information may be coupled with complex metadata structures
- users can be located anywhere and their nature, information needs, etc., may vary significantly
- there is no human intermediary and no physical collection, at least at the point of interaction
- a range of services, such as searching, filtering and downloading, as well as current awareness and selective dissemination of information services, may be provided
- there are many complex issues of information retrieval, access management, control of intellectual property rights, security, authentication, etc.
- in many cases, information is not owned; only a right to access is provided
- there may be several versions of the same information.

A recent review of 20 working digital libraries (Meyyappan, Chowdhury and Foo, 2000), from different parts of the world representing academic, special and public libraries shows the diversified collection of information resources. The review shows that the various information resources accessible to users are full-text articles, proceedings papers, CD-ROM databases, theses and dissertations, e-journals, e-books, examination papers, photographs, images of historic buildings, maps, audio, video, multimedia databases, collections of manuscripts, sound recordings, music collections, OPACs, union catalogues, etc. Some digital libraries, for example, the Networked Computer Science Technical Reference Library (NCSTRL) and the Networked Digital Library of Theses and Dissertations (NDLTD), contain collections of theses, dissertations and technical reports from various members' servers in different parts of the world. The California Digital Library (CDL) provides access to the collections of their nine campus libraries in an academic environment.

Search features of selected digital libraries

There are different categories of digital libraries, and their search and retrieval characteristics depend on their nature, information content, target users, and so on. Below we discuss the features of:

- digital libraries that deal with specific subjects and types of materials, NCSTRL and NDLTD
- a digital library that deals with non-textual information, the Alexandria Digital Library
- a digital library that deals with different types of materials, NZDL
- hybrid libraries that handle digital and well as traditional library materials, CDL and HeadLine.

NCSTRL

The Networked Computer Science Technical Reference Library is a digital collection of computer science research reports and papers made available for non-commercial use from a number of participating institutions and archives. Most of the NCSTRL institutions are universities that grant doctoral degrees in computer science or engineering, with some industrial or government research laboratories. The NCSTRL search page (Figure 8.1) allows users to search the collection. The various search features available here are shown in Table 8.1.

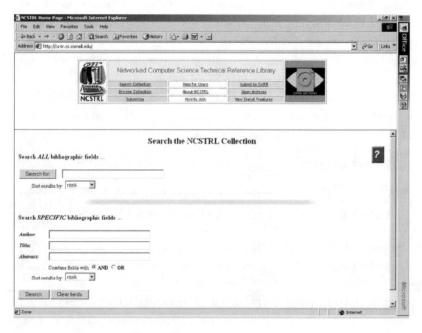

Fig. 8.1   *NCSTRL search screen*

Table 8.1 *Search and retrieval features of NCSTRL*

Feature	Explanation
Browse	User can browse records by all, one or a range of years; by author – by one or more letters; and from all or a chosen institution (from a drop-down box)
Search	'all', or a particular field, such as author or title can be selected
Boolean search	Boolean AND, OR operators are available to combine search terms
Truncation	All search terms are automatically right-truncated
Phrase search	Users can enter a phrase within quotes
Output	• number of records can be specified • records are ranked by score, or can be sorted by author, date, institution, or title • records contain brief information with hyperlinks • title and author are hyperlinked to full text • output format cannot be changed

The NCSTRL collection can be browsed by institution, by year, and by author (see Figure 8.2). A specific institution can be selected from a list, and a specific year, or a range of years, can be specified for browsing. For browsing by author, a particular letter, or range of letters may be chosen.

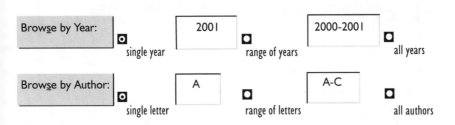

Select one or more institutions from this list:

All NCSTRL institutions	▲
Albert-Ludwigs-Universitaet Freiburg, Institut fuer Informatik	
Auburn University	
Boston University	▼

Fig. 8.2   *Browsing the NCSTRL collection*

Note: the URL for the NCSTRL has changed to **http://cs-tr.cs.cornell.edu/**. However, the old URL, **http://www.ncstrl.org**, takes users directly to the new URL.

NDLTD

The Networked Digital Library of Theses and Dissertations is a collection of electronic theses and dissertations (ETD). It started at Virginia Polytechnic Institute and State University, USA, and many institutions in the USA and overseas have joined the programme to form a federation. Users accessing the NDLTD website can search theses and dissertations available at any participating institution, or can search all the participating institutions. Figure 8.3 shows the NDLTD home page. Here users can choose a specific institution to search. Each institution has its own site: Figure 8.4 shows the ETD webpage of Virginia Polytechnic Institute and State University.

The collection can be browsed by author or searched with Infoseek (Figure 8.4). The alphabetical list of authors and titles of their theses is shown in Figure 8.5. There are two search interfaces for the ETD – the simple search interface (Figure 8.6) and the advanced interface (Figure 8.7).

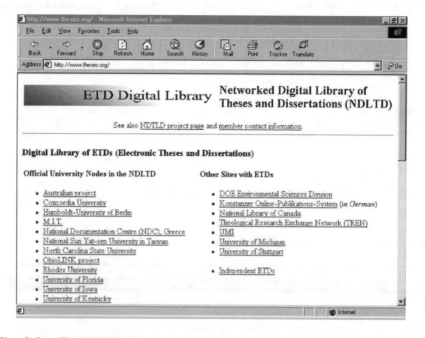

Fig. 8.3   *The NDLTD home page*

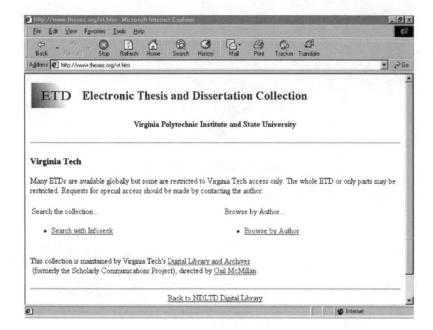

Fig. 8.4   *The Virginia Polytechnic Institute and State University ETD web page*

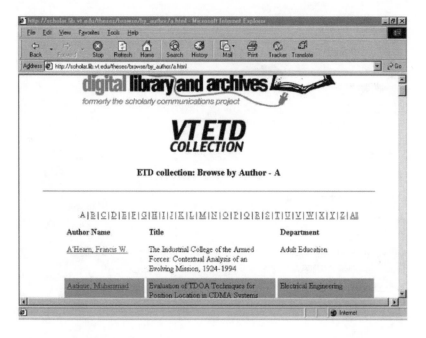

Fig. 8.5   *The ETD browse screen*

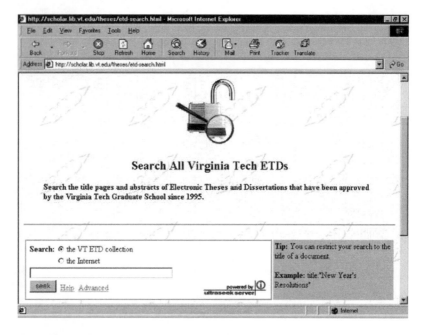

Fig. 8.6   *The ETD simple search interface*

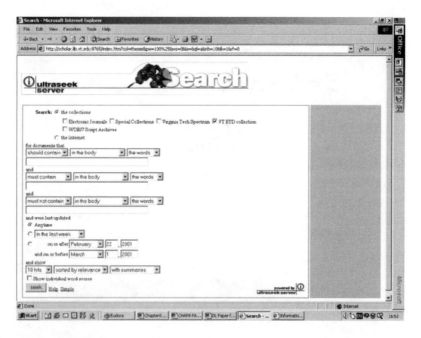

Fig. 8.7   *The ETD advanced search interface*

Table 8.2 shows the various search and retrieval features of the ETD. While searching, users can select a specific collection or can conduct searches across all the collections. However, when the latter option is taken, the number of hits can be high: for example, when a search on 'digital libraries' was conducted on all five collections, 5833 documents were retrieved; when only the Virginia Tech ETD was selected, the same search retrieved only 65 documents.

The ETD search interface varies according to the participating institution. For example, when we chose the MIT collection from the NDLTD home page (Figure 8.3), we obtained the MIT ETD search page (Figure 8.8), which is quite different from that of Virginia Tech (Figure 8.4).

Table 8.2 *Search and retrieval features of Virginia Tech ETD*

Feature	Explanation
One or all collections can be searched	Once the user selects a particular site, the collection can be browsed by author. Each collection has its own site and search interface
Search options	• specific collection or federated search • simple and advanced search • field search • search with InfoSeek or browse by author
Boolean search	'+' indicates that a search term must occur, and '–' that it must not. In the advanced search mode, there are the 'should contain', 'must contain' and 'must not contain' options.
Proximity search	No special operator; users can enter a phrase within quotes
Limiting search: by time	Users can limit their search by the date of approval; the limiting options are: days, weeks, months, year
Phrase and name search	Users can select to search for a word, a phrase or a name
Output	• output is ranked and can be sorted by relevance, date or title • the number of results and format (with or without summary) can be specified • author, department, abstract, files (number and format), and availability information is given

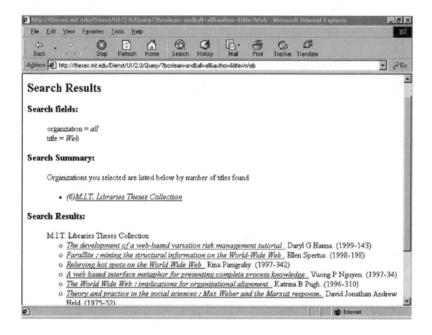

Fig. 8.8   *The search page for the MIT electronic theses collection*

Alexandria Digital Library (ADL)

ADL is the outcome of research funded by DLI-1 in the USA. The project began in 1995 with the development of a working digital library with collections of geographically referenced materials and services for accessing those collections. The Alexandria Digital Library Project is headquartered on the campus of the University of California at Santa Barbara. The materials held include maps, images and texts, and datasets in multimedia form in earth and social sciences. The ADL Catalog provides geospatial data and metadata in digital and hardcopy form. The coverage is worldwide but concentrated on southern California. Major digital collections include: DRGs (digital raster graphics: scanned US Geological Survey topographic maps) for California; SPOT satellite images for California; and scanned maps of foreign countries. Major metadata-only series include: Geodex (sheet-level records for mainly topographic maps, worldwide); frame-level records for aerial photography acquired from the NASA/Ames Research Center (mainly US); and scene-level records for Landsat Multispectral Scanner imagery (worldwide). Most items in the ADL Catalog are held by the Map and Imagery Laboratory; Geodex reflects holdings of other major map collections in California. The ADL Gazetteer allows users to search for geographic names, and searches can be restricted to particular types of features (e.g. to 'hydrographic features' or to 'lakes'). The ADL Gazetteer combines the US place names from the US Geological Survey's GNIS database, the non-US place names from the National Imagery and Mapping Agency's GNS database, and other gazetteer datasets. Figure 8.9 shows the ADL Map Browser, and Table 8.3 shows the various search and retrieval features of the ADL interface.

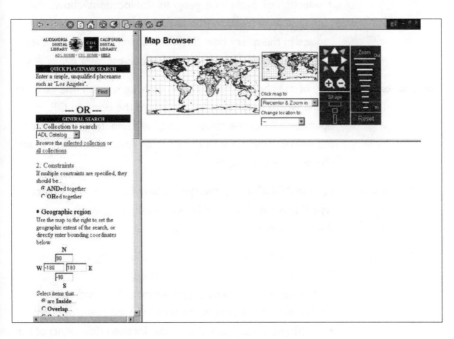

Fig. 8.9   *ADL Map Browser*

Table 8.3 *Search and retrieval features of ADL*

Features	Explanation
Map browser	users can pan and zoom a two-dimensional map of the world to locate their area(s) of interest
Search options	• users can search by geographic names, latitude and longitude, resource types (maps, photographs, etc.) and formats (online, offline, paper, etc.)

(continued)

Table 8.3 *(continued)*

Features	Explanation
	• users can search by originators: authors, publishers, etc.; assigned terms: subject headings and index terms assigned by the indexers; or free-text search: titles, abstracts, themes, and place names in the metadata
	• selection of 'Search on geographical locations' shows the geographical location (the latitude, longitude, etc.) of the place in the query box; 'Identifier search' can be searched by URL, ISBN, ADL Control Number, etc.
Boolean search	'Any of the above words' option finds items with one or more of the words in the box (equivalent to the Boolean OR operator); 'All of the above words' will find items with all of the words (equivalent to the Boolean AND operator); 'Exact phrase' is another option
Types of thesaurus	For the ADL Catalog, the type is based on the ADL object type thesaurus. For the ADL Gazetteer, the type is based on the ADL feature type thesaurus
Search results	Results of a query are displayed in the lower right-hand frame. Each item is represented by a short descriptive entry containing title (or name), type, format, date, and collection ID. For each result, users can select the following options: • 'highlight in map' will display the location (footprint) of the item in the Map Browser • 'complete description' will display the full metadata record of the item in the same frame • 'access/download' will display the access and download information in the same frame. For online items, hyperlinks are included for accessing the data; for offline items, contact information is provided. At the end of each listing of results, a report is included describing the query, the date, and the time it took the system to return the results. This information will be particularly useful if you print out or save the results for later referral.

NZDL

The New Zealand Digital Library project is a research programme at the University of Waikato whose aim is 'to develop the underlying technology for digital libraries and make it available publicly so that others can use it to create their own collections'. It provides access to several digital collections:

- reference collection: includes Arabic collection, Chinese collection, computer science technical reports and bibliographies, human–computer interaction bibliography, Project Gutenberg collection, and women's history and youth oral history collections
- humanitarian and UN collection: includes Food and Agricultural Organization (FAO) collection, collection of critical global issues, humanity development library, food and nutrition library, world environment library, virtual disaster library, and indigenous peoples and poverty alleviation collections
- demonstration collection: SCMS (School of Computer and Mathematical Sciences collection), language extraction demo, acronym extraction demo, and so on.

Greenstone digital library software, which is available free from NZDL, is used to provide search and browsing facilities for all the collections. The members of the NZDL project

> are actively working on techniques for creating, managing, and maintaining collections; extracting metadata from legacy documents; analysing library usage and user needs; Maori, Arabic and Chinese language systems; internationalising the library interface; optical music recognition and musical collections; novel interfaces for formulating queries and visualising results; novel interfaces for browsing metadata; text mining for keyphrases, acronyms, and other metadata; keyphrase extraction and phrase-based browsing; and other research topics.

Figure 8.10 shows the New Zealand Digital Library home page. Users need to select a specific collection; each collection has a different set of searching and browsing facilities (see Table 8.4).

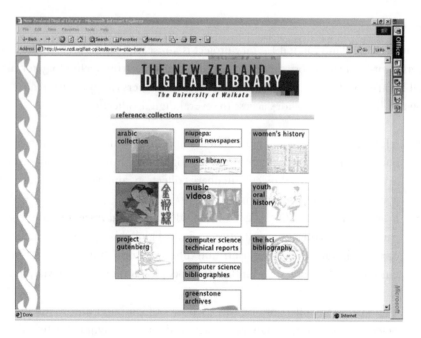

Fig. 8.10 *The NZDL home page*

Table 8.4 *Search and retrieval features of NZDL*

Features	Explanations
Browsing collections	Each collection has a different set of criteria for browsing, e.g., the computer science reports collection can be browsed from a list of ftp sites; the women's history collection can be browsed by titles, and so on
Search options	• For each collection there is a different set of search options, which vary from keyword search to searching through the 'Melody Index'. • Depending on the search collection, users can limit a search by titles, full text, photos, interviews, sections, paragraphs, and so on. • Users can click on a bookshelf icon for books on that subject. • Users can select the simple or advanced search mode.

(continued)

Table 8.4 *(continued)*

Features	Explanations
Boolean search	In the advanced search mode, search terms can be combined using Boolean AND, OR, NOT operators and parentheses; there are 'All the words' and 'Some words' options
Truncation	The preferences button on top of the page has two pairs of buttons: the first set controls case sensitivity, and the second set controls whether or not to ignore word endings (stemming)
Preferences	Users can change the search parameters including the language and interface format, by clicking 'Preferences'
Ranked output	If the user specifies only one term, documents will be ordered by its frequency of occurrence

California Digital Library

The California Digital Library (CDL) was founded in 1997. The Library is built on the extensive base of the University of California and is charged with the selection, building, management, and preservation of the University's shared collections of digital resources and applying new technologies to enhance sharing of the University's physical collections. CDL provides access to

- the Online Archive of California (OAC), a union database of digital descriptions of archival and manuscript collections from all of the UC campuses and from around California
- the Melvyl Catalog, records for materials in the libraries of the nine UC campuses, and some other libraries in California
- the California Periodicals Database, comprising the journal holdings of the nine UC campuses, and other libraries in California
- electronic journals
- a number of journal abstracting and indexing databases
- specialized and reference resources, such as the Web of Science, government data, and Encyclopedia Britannica online.

Figure 8.11 shows the CDL home page. By clicking on the 'Select a QuickLink' option, users are shown a list of all the various collections of CDL. Users can

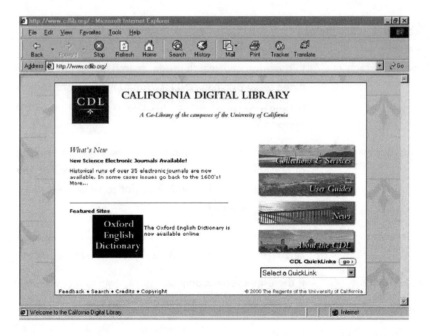

Fig. 8.11 *The CDL home page*

choose the 'directory of collections and services' link to search for a specific collection, such as electronic journals, databases, reference texts, etc. The following steps may be followed to browse the directory collections:

1 Select a broad topic
2 Select a format (electronic journal, database, etc.)
3 Select a Campus of interest (or no limit by campus)
4 Browse by title or narrower topic(s).

The various search and retrieval features of CDL are shown in Table 8.5.

Table 8.5 *Search and retrieval features of CDL*

Features	Explanations
Browse by selecting a topic	• The 8 main categories, general interest & references, history, social science, etc., have subcategories to browse through
	• Users can also choose the option for browsing through titles

(continued)

Table 8.5 *(continued)*

Features	Explanations
	• Browsing can be limited by format: electronic journals, databases, reference texts, etc., and library holdings
Search options	• Users can search the CDL directory of collections & services, and the CDL site • Users can search the CDL website excluding the digital resources • Users can search by keyword or by the exact beginning of a title • A search can be limited to a specific format, and/or to a specific library collection.
Boolean search	Boolean OR and NOT operators are not supported by the Searchlight system (the search tool used in CDL); AND is implied between each word.
Proximity search	Not available
Truncation	Users can use two truncation symbols: an asterisk (*) or the hash sign (#)
Limiting search	Users can choose one or more formats, and can select a particular library (the default is all the libraries) in the UC system
Query refinement	Users can revise a search by entering a new term(s) and/or changing the selected subject categories
Output	• results are categorised according to the source (databases, journals, Etexts, etc.), ranked by the no. of hits under each category • each record contains brief details of the document concerned and two options: 'more info' and a hyperlink • by clicking on the no. of hits, the user can see brief information on each output record with a hyperlink to the text version of the full document, its PDF format or the summary

(continued)

Table 8.5 *(continued)*

Features	Explanations
	• the source hyperlink takes the users to the particular collection (the URL) where they can enter a search expression in the search interface of the source. The search can be modified by choosing the appropriate options on the same output screen.

Figure 8.12 shows the output of a simple search on 'world wide web'. Search results are presented under various categories: Books, Journal Indexes , Electronic Journals, E-texts & Documents, Reference Resources, and Web Directories. The user can:

- link directly to a given resource by clicking on the 'Go to it now' button under a given entry
- click on the 'more information' link under a given entry to see details such as creator or publisher, dates of coverage, and links to tutorials where available
- examine and change the browse or search conditions.

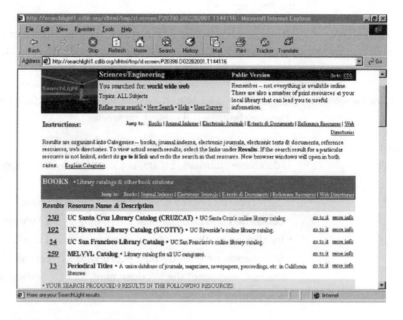

Fig. 8.12 *CDL search results*

HeadLine

The Hybrid Electronic Access and Delivery in the Library Networked Environment library project, funded by eLib, aims to design and implement a working model of the hybrid library in academic environments. It aims to provide users with a wide range of library resources, regardless of physical form, via a common web-based interface (Gambles, 2000). The subject focus is economics, finance, business and management, although the project aims to demonstrate portability of the model to other subject areas. The project began in January 1998 and is expected to end on 31 July 2001.

Although the digital library was not operational at the time of writing this book, the site provided a demonstration that is an example of what a 'typical' student user's session might involve. In this book we attempted to provide an overview of the PIE (personal information environment) of HeadLine, based on the demonstration version (Gambles, n.d.).

First the user logs in from the HeadLine PIE authentication screen, and then clicks on the 'Access the PIE' option (see Figure 8.13); the user's PIE, the default page, is displayed (see Figure 8.14). The top section of the PIE details the name of the page, the key to the buttons on the lower right-hand side of the

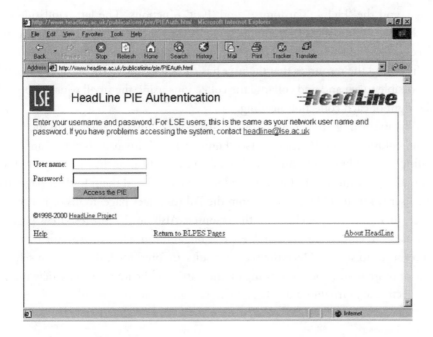

Fig. 8.13 The HeadLine log-in screen

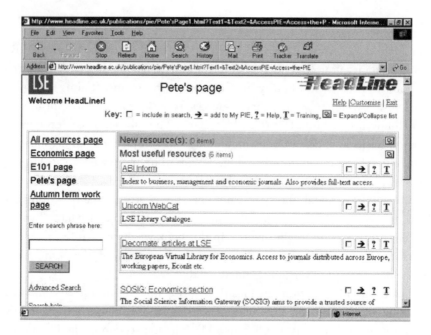

Fig. 8.14 *A sample HeadLine PIE*

page, and the 'Help', 'Customise' and 'Exit' functions. The left-hand side of each page within the PIE contains links to the other pages that the user can access. The right-hand side of the page includes the collections that the user has defined and the resources that the user has chosen to add to these collections. It is possible to expand and collapse the collections using the small square icon to the right of each collection heading.

The user can go to the 'All resources page' via a link that appears in the left-hand column of the PIE screen (see Figure 8.15) . This page includes an A-Z listing of all library resources and a subject classification listing. It acts as a source page from which the user can take items and add them to their page. If the user wants to add a resource from the 'All resources page' to his or her own page, he or she simply clicks on the resource. Also on the 'All resources page', the user can enter a simple search expression, and can select the specific type(s) of resource to search. Once the search results are presented, the user can select one or more items, and, depending on the nature of the item (book, article from an electronic journal or a database, etc.), can go ahead and use it.

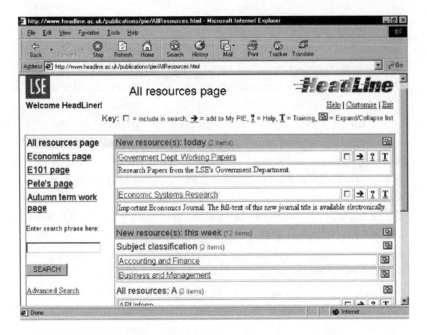

Fig. 8.15 *The HeadLine 'All resources page'*

Summary

In this chapter we discussed the basic characteristics of digital libraries, and described the features of six of these. Digital libraries vary in size, nature, contents, services, and so on. While some digital libraries provide simple search and retrieval facilities, others are more sophisticated. It is difficult to compare the digital libraries on a one-to-one basis, because of their differences in origin, objectives, content, target audience, etc. However, there are some common points that are worth noting. Chowdhury and Chowdhury (2000) studied the information retrieval features of 20 working digital libraries, which revealed the following points:

1   Common search features: very few digital libraries provide all the search facilities that are common in online search services and web search engines, such as keyword and phrase search, Boolean search, proximity and truncation, field-specific search, limiting search, and so on.
2   Searching through the indexes/terms dictionary: digital libraries expect users to begin their search by keying in words or phrases. Though some allow users to browse through the alphabetical lists of authors, titles, etc.,

provision for searching through terms dictionaries is not available.

3   Database/collection selection: a digital library may comprise several collections in the same or different locations. It may not be easy for a user to choose the most appropriate database/collection to search. In order to solve this problem, Dialog provides a master index, called DIALINDEX, which allows the user to key in a query and then the system, through the master index, shows how many hits each database has got for the given search.

4   Ranked output: some digital libraries produce ranked output, while others don't. However, the digital libraries studied do not indicate the criteria used for ranking the results.

5   Multimedia search: currently textual information forms a significant part of many digital libraries. Though some digital libraries, such as the ADL, have developed special techniques for handling multimedia information, such as digital video, and so on, most digital libraries use multimedia information as associated files that need to be searched through the associated text.

6   Natural language search: most digital libraries do not allow users to enter natural-language search queries. They expect users to combine the various search terms/phrases, with the appropriate Boolean and other search operators, to formulate the query.

7   Multilingual search and display: currently digital libraries do not search and display information in different languages.

8   Related queries: one of the major problems that users face in any information retrieval system, and more so in digital libraries, is that the entire process of searching and retrieval depends on the nature of the query formulated by users. However, information scientists have repeatedly shown that translating exact information requirements into an appropriate search formulation is not an easy task.

9   Database description: currently digital libraries give only a brief description of each collection, and so the user may find it difficult to select the appropriate database/collection. Online search services provide more detailed descriptions of databases through associated files, such as the Dialog blue sheets. Similarly detailed descriptions, available interactively from the search screen, of each database or collection, would be helpful to the users of digital libraries.

While digital library research and development activities are still very young, they are already a significant development. Much information that was earlier considered proprietary, and accessible to only certain categories of privileged users, is now available to all, and in many cases it is free. Although digital libraries differ in terms of their search interfaces and search and retrieval facilities, and sometimes users need to spend time becoming familiar with these, the prize they get at the end of a search session can be of immense importance – valuable information from remote locations, and often free. This represents a definite improvement in the information service environment, and a paradigm shift in the information industry.

Chapter 9
Issues and trends

Introduction

This book aimed to provide an overview of the various tools and techniques that can be used to search, retrieve and make the best use of the huge volume and variety of information available on the web. We have discussed search engines and directories, and subject gateways, the subject directories chosen and categorized by human experts in various subject domains, with a view to overcoming some problems of domain-independent directories on the web, such as Yahoo!.

The web is now used by various institutions to provide access to information: for example, libraries have web OPACs (Online Public Access Catalogues), database services now have web interfaces to their online databases, and various institutions have made their databases and other information resources accessible via the web. Chowdhury and Chowdhury (2001) discussed the features of such services. The web is also used by publishers who wish to make their electronic journals and electronic books easily available, and many digital libraries have been built over the past few years that allow users to access and use library resources through the web.

Reference and information services have long been the preserve of libraries and online search service providers, such as the Institute of Scientific Information, Dialog, and so on. However, the web has brought a tremendous change in the provision of reference and information services, some of which are run by libraries, but most are commercial ventures.

Search engines

Search engines are by far the largest and most frequently used tools for searching information on the web. As discussed in Chapter 3, search engines vary in terms of their size, characteristics, subject domain, and so on. A survey by Sullivan (2000), has shown how search engines have grown in size since the mid-1990s.

The size of the index of a search engine is an important determining factor. According to a recent survey by Sullivan (2000), Google has an index of 602 million web pages, followed by FAST (575 million pages), WebTop.com (500 million pages), AltaVista (350 million pages), Northern Light (300 million pages), Excite (250 million pages), Inktomi (110 million pages), and Go (InfoSeek) (50 million pages). However, Google is a special case. It has indexed 602 million pages, but because of the way Google uses link data, it can actually return listings for sites it has never visited. This gives it coverage of over 1.2 billion pages.

Some search engines have some special characteristics that make them more useful. A good example is Ask Jeeves.com, which allows users to ask a simple question, and either provides the answer to the question, or produces a list of predefined questions that are related to the question asked by the user. This is particularly useful for users with ill-defined questions, and it also allows users to learn more on related topics or related questions. It is expensive to build and maintain such sites, since it involves human expertise. The Ask Jeeves.com service has prompted information professionals to think more about getting involved in providing e-reference services (see p. 156).

Directories and subject gateways

Directories allow users to find web information resources by browsing through a hierarchy of categories and subcategories. Chapter 4 discussed the basic characteristics and features of web directories. Directories vary in terms of their size and their approaches to organizing information resources, and they provide much smaller search output than the major search engines. According to Sullivan (2000), Open Directory has a list of 325,000 categories that provides links to 2.2 million web pages (as of December 2000), LookSmart lists 200,000 categories providing links to 2 million web pages (as of August 2000), and NBCi (Snap) has 80,000 categories providing links to 1.5 million web pages.

Although web directories are very useful tools, they have two major problems. The first is caused by their fundamental approach to organizing the web resources: they do not follow any standard in creating their various categories and subcategories. As a result, it is sometimes difficult for the end-users to choose the correct category pertaining to a topic of search. The problem is multiplied for inter-disciplinary topics that may appear in more than one category in the hierarchy. The second problem is the difficulty inherent in categorizing all the possible disciplines in a manageable directory, which causes cross-, and often wrong, classification of subjects. Subject directories or gateways have been developed to alleviate these problems and to create directories more focused on specific disciplines. These subject directories, like the general web directories, provide both browse and good search facilities.

Digital libraries, e-journals and e-books

Chapter 8 discussed the basic characteristics of digital libraries, and their search and retrieval features. These vary significantly, and so users need to learn the various search tools and techniques in order to be able to search them effectively. The search interface of a digital library is particularly important since the interface is the only connection between a user and the library collections. In a traditional library, a user may talk to a human intermediary, walk and browse through the shelves or can pick materials from various locations. In the digital library the search interface is the only link between the user and the collections, and so the interface and the search and retrieval facilities should be as sophisticated and friendly as possible. Many digital libraries allow users to create a personal work space where they can store links to the information resources that they have found useful at a given instance. Zhao (1998) discusses the personal digital library (PDL), which acts as a front-end to other electronic library systems and manages the user's information needs. The main focus of the system is adaptive contents whereby users have their own personal and personalized databases. MyLibrary (Cohen et al., 2000) is a Cornell University Library initiative to provide personalized library services to their students, faculty, and staff on the basis of a focus group study to gauge library users. The project has two components, MyLink and MyUpdate. MyLink enables users to save useful information resource links that they have found themselves or that have been suggested by librarians via a targeted notification in their personal space. Users can access this personal space from anywhere. MyUpdate periodically queries the online catalogue and notifies the users, according to their predefined needs.

HeadLine is developing the personal information environment (PIE), which allows users to create their personal collection by selecting the results of a search and storing the information on their personal web pages. The PIE uses portal-type technology to present an information environment that is personalized to the user's needs and allows user customization. This project presents users with pages of resources relevant to their courses/department. PIE users are also provided with an 'All resources' page which contains links to all the resources to which their library provides access. Users can create their own lists of resources on their own pages.

Chowdhury and his associates (Meyyappan et al., 2001a, 2001b) have recently proposed a digital work environment (DWE) that aims to provide users with the appropriate information needed to accomplish a particular task. The system is based on an analysis of the various tasks of users in an academic institution. The basic tenet is that the users need not know about the existence (or non-existence) of a particular information source, nor do they need to formulate a query to look for an information source. The DWE expects a user to identify a particular task that he/she wants to accomplish at a particular moment, and the system, based on its knowledge about the given user as well as of the various information resources and their suitability to a particular task, will take the user to the appropriate source of information.

Chapter 7 described the nature and characteristics of e-journals and e-books. There are various ways of accessing, browsing and searching e-journals, and the search and retrieval features of systems providing access vary significantly. Many digital libraries also provide access to e-journals and e-books by linking to the search interface of the journal publisher. If the journal is subscribed through an aggregator, then the user is taken to the search interface provided by that aggregator. In either case, the user can browse issue by issue, by author or title, or can use the subject search facilities. The search facilities vary from one system to another.

There are different types of e-books, both electronic versions of printed books, which can be accessed via the publisher's web interface (for example Britannica.com, Infoplease.com, or through digital libraries), and books that are published solely in electronic format. These can be downloaded from the publisher or online bookseller, and can be read using software on computer or on a dedicated handheld device.

These recent developments are bringing tremendous changes in the way we buy and read books and manage our own personal libraries.

Online reference and information services

As discussed in Chapter 6, many web-based reference and information services are now available, provided not only by libraries, but also by individuals and companies. This means that users need not go to a specific library to obtain a reference service, and the service is not restricted by the collection of a given library (Sherman, 2000). Users can go to a particular site and can search for information on their own, as is the case with InfoPlease or Britannica.com, or can ask a question that will be answered by a librarian or an expert. Though the quality, and cost, of services varies, the opportunities for end-users are enormous.

In a comparative study of three web-based reference services, Ask Jeeves, Electric Library, and Information Please, Sherman (2000) noted:

- Ask Jeeves is useful for complex questions, and is a good choice for searchers that lack Boolean or other searching skills, because of its strong natural language parser and question-and-answer template structure.
- Electric Library is an excellent choice for a serious researcher in need of timely content from a wide array of otherwise unavailable sources.
- Information Please is an excellent tool for students and other researchers, as an authoritative source of facts and pointers for further investigation.

Lankes et al. (2000) have pointed out that 'the reference librarian in the new millennium will need the ability to read the situation a user is in and find the right information for that situation'. In addition, to keep pace with the rapid developments of web-based reference and information services provided by non-library organizations, many library and information science professionals have now turned their attention to the provision of e-reference services. Oder and Weissman (2001) suggest that 'The year 2000 brought the advent of live reference. Several libraries, especially academic ones, have used or adapted chat or commercial call center software to communicate with surfers in real time and send web resources to their browser'.

Public libraries throughout the UK are working together to provide Ask a Librarian (see p. 81). This service uses e-mail communication facilities to receive users' queries, route them to a library and finally send users their answers. Another interesting development related to electronic reference services is the establishment of the CDRS (Collaborative Digital Reference Service) Project in the US. The idea of this project was originated at a conference entitled 'Building the Virtual Reference Desk in a 24/7 World', co-sponsored by the Library of Congress and OCLC (Saunders, 2001). The objective of CDRS is to provide a 'professional reference service to researchers any time anywhere, through an international, digital network of libraries and related institutions'. Through CDRS, an end-user may ask a question and receive an answer from a librarian working through a participating member organization. Libraries can assist their users by connecting to the CDRS to send questions that are answered by the expert staff and collections of CDRS member institutions from around the world. In November 2000 the Library of Congress finished the final test of the CDRS's Phase 3, in which more than 50 members had participated (Saunders, 2001). Several libraries in the US have looked to consortia to launch regional reference services: for example, consortia around Los Angeles (the 24/7 Reference Project at Metropolitan Cooperative Library System) and San Francisco (Bay Area Libraries Project) have begun training librarians and testing software for live reference service (Oder and Weissman, 2001).

A number of publications have come out recently describing many digital reference services, the corresponding benefits and so on. See, for example, Lankes (2000) and Oder and Weissman (2001). Two up-to-date bibliographies on digital reference services are now available online (Hadid, n.d.; Sloan, n.d.).

Conclusion

So, where do all these exciting developments lead us to? Traditionally the activities related to the organization, searching and dissemination of information have been the core of the library and information profession. However, we have shown that library and information professionals are not alone in providing electronic reference and information services. Many dotcoms are now in this business, which is moving very fast. For end-users this is an exciting time, as these new information services are providing fast, effective and often free electronic information services. Developments in the library and information service sector have not kept up, and most services are still limited to utilizing merely the communication facilities of the internet, mainly e-mail. The major reason for this slow progress may be attributed to lack of funds for the new venture, compared with what is available for commercial ventures. Another reason is the lack of technical capabilities of some library and information professionals, many of whom are finding it difficult to keep pace with the rapid developments in the internet and the web, let alone the underlying technologies; again funding is a factor. We need more training and expertise in the internet, web and related technologies in order to be better equipped to provide better information services, as has long been the mission of the library and information profession.

References

ARL (n.d.) *Directory of scholarly electronic journals and academic discussion lists* http://arl.cni.org/scomm/edir/

ARL (1999) The ARL Directory of Electronic Journals, Newsletters and Academic Discussion Lists (1999), *Library Hi Tech*, **17** (1), 17–25.

Arms, W. Y. (2000) *Digital libraries*, The MIT Press.

Baeza-Yates, R. and Ribeiro-Neto, B. (1999) *Modern information retrieval*, Addison-Wesley.

Bates, M. J. (1998) Indexing and access for digital libraries and the Internet: human, database, and domain factors, *Journal of the American Society for Information Science*, **49** (13), 1185–205.

Bergman, M. (n.d.) *The deep web: surfacing hidden value*, BrightPlanet. http://www.brightplanet.com/

Borgman, C. (1999) What are digital libraries? Competing visions, *Information Processing and Management*, **35**, 227–43.

Bradley, P. (1999) *The advanced Internet searcher's handbook*, Library Association Publishing.

Campbell, D. (2000) Australian subject gateways: political and strategic issues, *Online Information Review*, **24** (1), 73–7.

Chowdhury, G. G (1999a) *Introduction to modern information retrieval*, Library Association Publishing.

Chowdhury, G. G. (1999b) Template mining for information extraction from digital documents, *Library Trends,* **48** (1), 1999, 181–207.

Chowdhury, G. G. and Chowdhury, S. (1999) Digital library research: major issues and trends, *Journal of Documentation*, **55** (4), 409–48.

Chowdhury, G. G. and Chowdhury, S. (2000) An overview of the information retrieval features of twenty digital libraries, *Program,* **34** (4), 341–73.

Chowdhury, G. G. and Chowdhury, S. (2001) *Searching CD-ROM and online information sources*, Library Association Publishing.

Clarke, S. J. (1998) Search engines for the world wide web: an evaluation of recent development. In Iyer, H. (ed.), *Electronic resources: use and user behaviour,* Haworth Press, 81–93.

Client/server (n.d.) *Whatis?com*
http://whatis.techtarget.com/definition/0,281893,sid9_gci211796,00.html

Cohen, S., Fereira, J., Horne, A., Kibbee, B., Mistlebauer, H. and Smith, A. (2000) MyLibrary: personalized electronic services in the Cornell University library, *D-Lib Magazine*, **6** (4)
http://www.dlib.org/dlib/April00/mistlebauer 04mistlebauer.html

Cookie basics (n.d.) *How Stuff Works*
http://www.howstuffworks.com/cookie1.htm

Courtois, M. P. and Michael, W. B. (1999) Results ranking in web search engines, *Online*, **23** (3), 39–46.

Dempsey, L. (2000) The subject gateway: experiences and issues based on the emergence of the Resource Discovery Network, *Online Information Review*, **24** (1), 8–23.

Electronic journals: a selected resource guide (n.d.)
http://www.harrassowitz.de/top_resources/ejresguide.html

Fecko, M. B. (1997) *Electronic resources: access and issues*, Bowker-Saur.

Fischer, T. and Neuroth, H. (2000) SSG–FI: special subject gateways to high quality internet resources for scientific users, *Online Information Review*, **24** (1), 64–8.

Fox, E. A. (1999) Digital libraries initiative (DLI) projects 1994–1999, *Bulletin of the American Society for Information Science*, **26**, 7–11.

Gambles, A. (2000) Put yourself in the PIE – the HeadLine personal information environment, *D-Lib Magazine*, **6** (4).

Gambles, A. (n.d.) *Demonstration, building on the 'Basic Idea' for the HeadLine PIE*
http://www.headline.ac.uk/publications/pie/

Gladney, H. H., Fox, E. A., Ahmed, Z., Asany, R., Belkin, N.J. and Zemankova, M. (1994) 'Digital library: gross structure and requirements: report from a March 1994 workshop'.
http://www.csdl.tamu.edu/DL94/paper/fox.html

Glossbrenner, A. and Glossbrenner, E. (1999) *Search engines for the world wide web*, 2nd edn, Peachpit Press.

Granum, G. and Barker, P. (2000) An easier way to search online engineering resources, *Online Information Review*, **24** (1), 78–82.

Green, D. (2000) The evolution of web searching, *Online Information Review*, **24** (2), 124–37.

Griffin, S. M. (1999) Digital Libraries Initiative, Phase 2: fiscal year 1999 awards, *D-Lib Magazine*, **5** (7/8).
http://www.dlib.org/dlib/july999/07griffin.html

Hadid, P. (n.d.) Web-based reference services
http://www.multnomah.lib.or.us/lib/products/digref/resources.html

Hardin, V. (n.d.) The myths of electric butterflies
http://www.geocities.com/Paris/LeftBank/4266/WHATISANEBOOK. html

Harrassowitz (n.d.) Electronic journals: a selected resource guide
http://www.harrassowitz.de/top_resources/ejresguide.html

Heery, R. (2000) Information gateways: collaboration on content, *Online Information Review*, **24** (1), 40–5.

Hiom, D. (2000) SOSIG: an Internet hub for the social sciences, business and law, *Online Information Review*, **24** (1), 54–8.

Hock, R. (1998) How to do field search in web search engines, *Online*, **22** (3), 18–22.

Hock, R. (1999) Web search engines: features and commands, *Online*, **23** (3), 24–8.

How internet search engines work (n.d.) *How Stuff Works*
http://www.howstuffworks.com/search-engine.htm

How ports work (n.d.) *How Stuff Works*
http://www.howstuffworks.com/web-server5.htm

Hsieh-Yee, I. (1998) The retrieval power of selected search engines: how well do they address general reference questions and subject questions? In Iyer, H. (ed.) *Electronic resources: use and user behaviour*, Haworth Press, 27–47.

Huber, C. F (2000) Electronic journal publishers: electronic journal aggregators
http://www.library.ucsb.edu/istl/00-summer/huber-chart-3.html

Hudson, L. and Windsor, L. (1998) Providing access to electronic journals: the Ohio University experience, *Against the Grain*, **10** (3), 16–18.

Hume, C. (2000) Internet search engines and robots: what they are and how to use them. In Thomas, A. R. and Shearer, J E. (eds), *Internet searching and indexing: the subject approach*, Haworth Press, 29–45.

Jones, D. (1999) Collection development in the digital library. In Stern, D. (ed.) *Digital libraries: philosophies, technical design considerations, and example scenarios*, Haworth Press, 27–37.

Jones, W. (1998) Preface to the special issue on E-serials: publishers, libraries, users, and standards, (Part 1), *The Serials Librarian*, **33** (1/2), xv–xvi.

Koch, T. (2000) Quality-controlled subject gateways: definitions, typologies, empirical overview, *Online Information Review*, **24** (1), 24–34.

Lancaster, F. W. (1995) The evolution of electronic publishing, *Library Trends*, **43** (4), 518–27.

Lankes, D. et al. (eds) (2000) *Digital reference service in the new millennium: planning, management, and evaluation*, Neal-Schuman.

Lee, S. and Morris, W. (2000) Making friends with e-journals, *Library Association Record*, **102** (7), 392–3.

Lesk, M. (1997) *Practical digital libraries: books, bytes, and bucks*, Morgan Kaufmann.

Lesk, M. (1999) Perspectives on DLI-2: growing the field, *D-Lib Magazine*, **5** (7/8)
http://www.dlib.org/dlib/july99/07lesk.html

Lincicum, S. (n.d.) Cataloging documentation on the web
http://libweb.uoregon.edu/~catdept/tools/catdoc.html

Luther, J. (1998) Full text journal subscriptions: an evolutionary process
http://www.arl.org:591/luther.html

Machovec, G. (1997) Electronic journal market overview: March 1997
http://www.coalliance.org/reports/ejournal.htm

MacLeod, R. (2000) Promoting a subject gateway: a case study from EEVL (Edinburgh Engineering Virtual Library), *Online Information Review*, **24** (1), 59–63.

Marchionini, G. and Fox, E. (1999) Editorial: progress toward digital libraries: augmentation through integration, *Information Processing and Management*, **35**, 219–25.

McKay, S. C. (1999) Accessing electronic journals, *Database*
http://www.onlineinc.com/database/DB1999/mckay4.html

McKierman, G. (1999) Points of view: conventional and 'neo-conventional' access and navigation in digital collections, *Journal of Internet Cataloging*, **2** (1) 23–41.

McKnight, C. (1997) Electronic journals: what do users think of them?
http://www.dl.ulis.ac.jp/ISDL97/proceedings/mcknight.htm

Meyyappan, N., Chowdhury, G. and Foo, S. (2000) A review of the status of twenty digital libraries, *Journal of Information Science*, **26** (5), 331–47.

Meyyappan, N., Chowdhury, G. G. and Foo, S. (2001a) Use of a digital work environment prototype to create a user-centered university digital library, *Journal of Information Science*, **27** (4), 249–64.

Meyyappan, N., Chowdhury, G. G. and Foo, S. (2001b) An architecture of a user-centred digital library for the academic community. In Chen, C. C. (ed.), *Global digital library development in the new millennium: fertile ground for distributed cross-disciplinary collaboration, NIT 2001: 12th International Conference on New Information Technology*, Tsinghua University Press.

Miller, R. G. (1999) Electronic journals and the scholarly communication process: present and future. In Ching-Chih Chen (ed.), *IT and global digital library development*, MicroUse Information, 293–300.

Missingham, R. (2000) Portals down under: discovery in the digital age, *Econtent,* **23** (2), 41–8.

Mogge, D. (1999) Seven years of tracking electronic publishing: the ARL Directory of Electronic Journals, Newsletters and Academic Discussion Lists, *Library Hi Tech*, **17** (1)
http://www.emerald.library.com/brev/23817ac1.html

Neal, James G. (1997) The use of electronic scholarly journals: models of analysis and data drawn from the Project Muse experience at Johns Hopkins University, *Scholarly Communication and Technology, conference organized by the Andrew W. Mellon Foundation, at Emory University, April 24–25, 1997*
http://www.arl.org/scomm/scat/neal.html

Nicholson, S. (1998) A proposal for categorization and nomenclature for web search tools. In Iyer, H. (ed.), *Electronic resources: use and user behaviour,* Haworth Press, 9–28.

Notess, G. N. (1999) Search engines in the Internet age, *Online*, **23** (3), 20–2.

Oder, N. and Weissman, S. (2001) The shape of e-reference, *Library Journal*, **126** (2), 46–50.

Oppenheim, C. and Smithson, D. (1999) What is a hybrid library?, *Journal of Information Science*, **25** (2), 97–112.

Pack, T. (2000) Human search engines: the next killer app?, *Econtent*, **23** (6), 16–22.
http://www.ecmag.net/

Pinfield, S., Eaton, J., Edwards, C., Russell, R., Wissenburg, A. and Wynne, P. (1998) Realizing the hybrid library, *D-Lib Magazine*
http://www.dlib.org/dlib/october98/10pinfield.html

Porteous, J. (1997) Plugging into electronic journals, *Nature*, **389**, 137–8.

Poulter, A., Hiom, D. and Tseng, G. (2000) *The library and information professional's guide to the internet*, 3rd edn, Library Association Publishing.

Poulter, A., Tseng, G. and Sargent, G. (1999) *The library and information professional's guide to the world wide web*, Library Association Publishing.

Price, A. (2000) NOVAGate: a Nordic gateway to electronic resources in the forestry, veterinary and agricultural sciences, *Online Information Review*, **24** (1), 69–72.

Raitt, D. (1999) European developments in digital libraries. In Ching-Chih Chen (ed.), *IT and global digital library development*, MicroUse Information, 345–56.

Rusbridge, C. (1998) Towards the hybrid library, *D-Lib Magazine*
http://www.dlib.org/dlib/july98/rusbridge/07rusbridge.html

Saunders, L. (2001) IT report from the field: building the virtual reference desk, *Information Today*, **18** (3)
http://www.infotoday.com/it/mar01/saunders.htm

Schoonbaert, D. (1998) Biomedical journals and the world wide web, *The Electronic Library*, **16** (2), 95–103.

Search engine resources (n.d.)
http://www.webpromotion.co.uk/searchengines.htm

Server (n.d.) *Whatis?com*
http://whatis.techtarget.com/definition/0,289893,sid0_gci212964,00.html

Sherman , C. (1999) The future of web search, *Online*, **23** (3), 54–61.

Sherman, C. (2000) Reference resources on the web, *Online*, **24** (1), 52–6.

Sloan, B. (n.d.) Digital reference services: a bibliography
http://www.lis.uiuc.edu/%7Eb-sloan/digiref.html

Sonnenreich, W. and Macinta, M. (1998) *Web developer.com: guide to search engines*, John Wiley.

Sullivan, D. (2000). Search engine sizes
http://www.searchenginewatch.com/

Sullivan, D. (n.d.) Search engine watch
http://www.searchenginewatch.com/facts/index.html

Tyner, R. (n.d.) *Sink or swim: Internet search tools & techniques*
http://www.lboro.ac.uk/library/sink.html

Vicki, R. and Winograd, T. (1995) Working assumptions about the digital library (Stanford Digital Library Working paper)
http://wwwdiglib.stanford.edu/diglib/WP/PUBLIC/Doc10.html

Vizine-Goetz, D. (1997) Conceptual ordering of electronic document collections. In: *The 34th Annual Clinic on Library Applications of Data Processing, Talk on Visualizing Subject Access for 21st Century Information Resources*, University of Illinois, March 2–4
ftp://ftp.rsch.oclc.org/pub/vizine/dpc_at_uofi/
Waters, D. J. (1998) What are digital libraries? *CLIR Issues*, 4
http://www.clir.org/pubs/issues/issues04.html#dlf/
Web server (n.d.) *Whatis?com*
http://whatis.techtarget.com/definition/0,289893,sid9_gci213606,00.html
Zhao, D. (1998) The personal digital library. In *ELINOR: electronic library project*, Bowker-Saur for the British Library, 97–103.

Websites

Alexandria Digital Library
http://www.alexandria.ucsb.edu/
AllExperts.com
http://www.allexperts.com/
AltaVista
http://www.altavista.com/
Amazon.com
http://www.amazon.com
AOL Anywhere
http://search.aol.com/
AOL Kids Only
http://www.aol.com/netfind/kids/
Argus Clearinghouse
http://www.clearinghouse.net/
Ariadne
http://www.ariadne.ac.uk/
Ask a Librarian
http://www.earl.org.uk/ask/
Ask Auntie Nolo
http://www.nolo.com/auntie/
Ask Jeeves
http://www.ask.com/
AskMe
http://www1.askme.com/

Audiogalaxy
 http://www.audiogalaxy.com/
Barnes & Noble.com
 http://www.bn.com/
Bartleby Reference
 http://www.bartleby.com/reference/
Biz/ed, the Business and Economics Information Gateway
 http://www.bized.ac.uk/
BIOME
 http://biome.ac.uk
Blackwell's Electronic Journal Navigator
 http://navigator.blackwell.co.uk/
Britannica.com
 http://www.britannica.com/
BUBL Journals
 http://www.bubl.ac.uk/
BUBL Link
 http://link.bubl.ac.uk/linksearch/
California Digital Library
 http://www.cdlib.org/
Cnet Search.com
 http://www.search.com/
Cooperative Digital Reference Service
 http://lcweb.loc.gov/rr/digiref/
Copernic
 http://www.copernic.com/
Dialog Alerts
 http://www.dialog.com/info/support/alerts/
D-Lib Forum
 http://www.dlib.org/
Dogpile
 http://www.dogpile.com/
Earl: the consortium for public library networking
 http://www.earl.org.uk/
eBooks
 http://e-books.org/

EBSCO Online
http://www.ebsco.com/ess/services/online.stm/
EEVL, Edinburgh Engineering Virtual Library
http://www.eevl.ac.uk/infosheet.doc/
Electric Library
http://www.elibrary.com/
eLib: the Electronic Libraries Programme
http://www.ukoln.ac.uk/services/elib/
Elsevier's Contents Direct Service
http://www.elsevier.com/
EELS, Engineering E-Library, Sweden
http://eels.lub.lu.se/
Excite
http://www.excite.com/
FAST Search
http://www.alltheweb.com/
FIND/SVP
http://askus.findsvp.com/
Google
http://www.google.com/
HeadLine: Hybrid Electronic Access and Delivery in the Library Networked Environment
http://www.headline.ac.uk
HighWire Press
http://highwire.stanford.edu/
HotBot
http://www.hotbot.com/
Hypertext markup language
http://www.w3c.org/MarkUp/
IDEAL, International Digital Electronic Access Library
http://www.idealibrary.com/
Indiainfo.com
http://indiafocus.indiainfo.com/
InfoGrid
http://www.infogrid.com/
Information Please
http://www.infoplease.com/

Inforocket.com
   http://www.inforocket.com/
InfoSeek Express
   http://express.infoseek.com/
Ingenta
   http://www.ingenta.com/
Intelliseek
   http://www.profusion.com/
Internet Library for Librarians
   http://www.itcompany.com/inforetriever/
IPL (Internet Public Libraries) Reading Room Serials
   http://www.ipl.org/
ISI: fully integrated e-information solutions
   http://www.isinet.com/
Japanese search engines
   http://www.atrium.com/
JSTOR
   http://www.jstor.org/
KidsClick
   http://sunsite.berkeley.edu/KidsClick!/
Lexibot
   http://www.lexibot.com/transition.asp/
Location Power
   http://www.locationpower.com/se.htm
LookSmart
   http://www.looksmart.com/
Lycos
   http://www.lycos.com/
Magellan
   http://magellan.excite.com/
Mamma
   http://www.mamma.com/
Mediaeater Reference Desk
   http://www.mediaeater.com/easy-access/ref.html
Metacrawler
   http://www.metacrawler.com/

Moreover
   http://w.moreover.com/
Mosaique
   http://www.mosaique.net/
MP3.com
   http://www.mp3.com/
MSN
   http://www.msn.com/
NCSTRL, Networked Computer Science Technical Reference Library
   http://cs-tr.cs.cornell.edu/
Net.Journal Directory
   http://www.hermograph.com/njd/njd.htm
Networked Digital Library of Theses and Dissertations, NDLTD
   http://www.theses.org/
NewsIndex
   http://www.newsindex.com/
New Zealand Digital Library, NZDL
   http://www.nzdl.org/
Nielsen NetRatings
   http://www.nielsen-netratings.com/
Northern Light
   http://www.northernlight.com/
NOVAGate, Nordic Gateway to Information in Forestry, Veterinary and Agricultural Sciences
   http://novagate.nova-university.org/
Nuvomedia
   http://www.nuvomedia.com/
NZDL (New Zealand Digital Library)
   http://www.nzdl.org/cgi-bin/library/
OMNI: the UK's gateway to high quality Internet resources in health and medicine
   http://omni.ac.uk/about/background.html
Oregon State University Virtual Libraries
   http://osu.orst.edu/aw/promote/register/libraries.htm
Professional City.com
   http://www.professionalcity.com/
Project MUSE: scholarly journals online
   http://muse.jhu.edu/

Research-It!
    http://www.itools.com/research-it/
ScienceDirect
    http://www.sciencedirect.com/
Social Science Information Gateway, SOSIG
    http://www.sosig.ac.uk/
SoftBook Press
    http://www.softbook.com/
SwetsnetNavigator
    http://www.SwetsnetNavigator.com/
TiARA
    http://www.tiara.com.sg/
Universal Library
    http://www.ul.cs.cmu.edu/
University of California, Berkeley Digital Library Project
    http://elib.cs.berkeley.edu/
Web Crawler
    http://www.webcrawler.com/
Web Help
    http://www.webhelp.com/home/
Webopedia
    http://webopedia.internet.com/TERM/e/electronic_book.html
Wiley Book Notification Service
    http://www.wiley.com/promotion/wbns/
World Wide Web Virtual Library (WWW Virtual Library)
    http://www.vlib.org/
Yahoo!
    http://www.yahoo.com/
Yahooligans
    http://www.yahooligans.com/

Index